Toolkit

Corporate Transformation To Improve Productivity and Innovation

2010 ' Corporate Turnaround Centre

Author: Dr. Michael Teng

Published in 2011 by

Corporate Turnaround Centre Pte Ltd.

Printed in Singapore

By Mentor Media Ltd

2010' Corporate Turnaround Centre

TABLE OF CONTENTS

MODULE #2 – PHASE ONE: BREAKING THE BOTTLENECK: SURGERY: Focus on Productivity

MODULE #3 – PHASE TWO: BREAKING THE BOTTLENECK: RESUSCITATION Part I: FOCUS ON PRODUCTIVITY + INNOVATION

MODULE #4 – ULTIMATE INTERNET MARKETING:

FOCUS ON PRODUC TIVITY + INNOVATION

MODULE #5 – PHASE TWO (continued) OF BREAKING THE BOTTLENECK: RESUSCITATION Part II:

FOCUS ON PRODUCTIVITY + INNOVATION

MODULE #6 – PHASE THREE: BREAKING THE BOTTLENECK: THERAPY Part I: FOCUS ON INNOVATION

MODULE #7 – OFFICE POLITICS/TEAMWORK

MODULE #8 – PHASE THREE (Continued): BREAKING THE BOTTLENECK: THERAPY Part II
FOCUS ON INNOVATION

MODULE #9 – CORPORATE WELLNESS: ULTIMATE CORPORATE TRANSFORMATION [TM] INDEX = OUTPUT/INPUT @ INNOVATION CULTURE

MODULE #10 – TRANSFORM YOURSELF: CHANGING MINDSET

MODULES #11 and #12 – PRACTICAL SESSIONS

SUMMARY AND CONCLUSION

ENHANCING PRODUCTIVITY INNOVATIVELY (EPI) - SUBSTAINABLE ECO SYSTEM

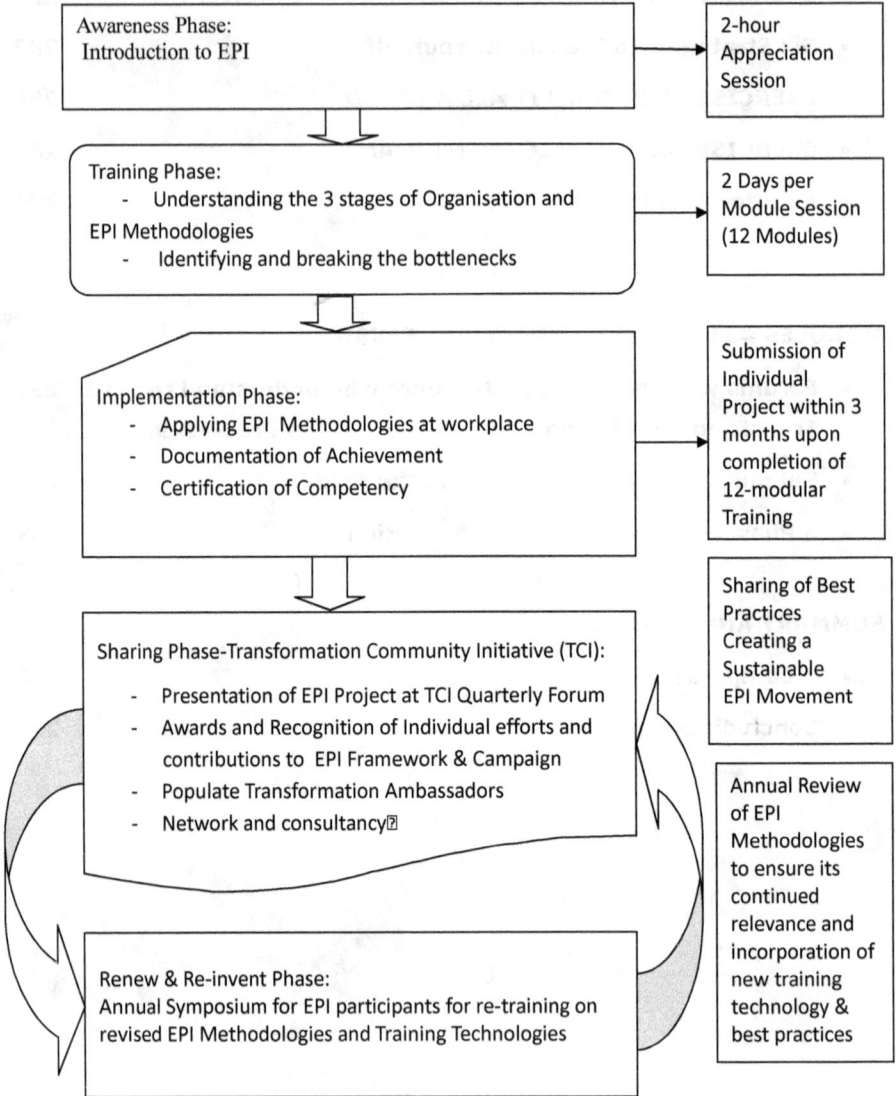

Awareness Phase: Introduction to EPI	2-hour Appreciation Session
Training Phase: - Understanding the 3 stages of Organisation and EPI Methodologies - Identifying and breaking the bottlenecks	2 Days per Module Session (12 Modules)
Implementation Phase: - Applying EPI Methodologies at workplace - Documentation of Achievement - Certification of Competency	Submission of Individual Project within 3 months upon completion of 12-modular Training
Sharing Phase-Transformation Community Initiative (TCI): - Presentation of EPI Project at TCI Quarterly Forum - Awards and Recognition of Individual efforts and contributions to EPI Framework & Campaign - Populate Transformation Ambassadors - Network and consultancy	Sharing of Best Practices Creating a Sustainable EPI Movement
Renew & Re-invent Phase: Annual Symposium for EPI participants for re-training on revised EPI Methodologies and Training Technologies	Annual Review of EPI Methodologies to ensure its continued relevance and incorporation of new training technology & best practices

2010 ' Corporate Turnaround Centre

About the Author

Dr. Teng is widely recognized as a turnaround CEO in Asia by the news media. He has been interviewed on the international media on many occasions on the subject of corporate turnaround and transformation as well as Internet marketing such as the Malaysian Business Radio, BFM 89-9, News Radio FM 93.8, Malaysian Business Radio, Edge Radio (USA), the Channel News Asia, the Boss Magazine, Economic Bulletin, the Today, World Executive Digest, Lianhe ZaoPao, StarBiz and the Straits Times. His online seminars are broadcasted globally by Success University and SkyquestCom to 120 countries.

Dr. Mike Teng is the author of a best-selling book *"Corporate Turnaround: Nursing a Sick Company Back to Health"*, in 2002 which is also translated into the Bahasa, Indonesia and Mandarin. His book is endorsed by management guru Professor Philip Kotler and business tycoons Mr. Oei Hong Leong and Dr. YY Wong. He subsequently authored more than nineteen management books. Three of the books are on Internet marketing.

Dr. Teng is currently the Managing Director of Corporate Turnaround Centre Pte Ltd (www.corporateturnaroundcentre.com) which provides corporate training and management advisory services in Singapore, Malaysia, Vietnam, Ghana, etc. He is the national trainer appointed by the Singapore government to train displaced senior managers and deploy them to run SMEs.

He has more than 29 years of experience in starting new plants, strategic planning, and operational management responsibilities in the Asia Pacific region. Of these, he held Chief Executive Officer positions for 19 years in multi-national and publicly listed companies. He was the CEO of a U.S. MNC based in Singapore for ten years. He spearheaded the turnaround of several troubled companies. He also advised several boards of directors of publicly-listed companies.

Dr. Teng served as an Executive Council member for fourteen years and the last four years as the President of the Marketing Institute of Singapore (2000 – 2004), the national marketing association. He was on the advisory board member to Business School, National University of Singapore and School of Business, Singapore Polytechnic as well as the Doctoral Program, University of South Australia.

Dr. Teng holds a Doctorate in Business Administration (DBA) from the University of South Australia, a Master of Business Administration (MBA) and Bachelor of Mechanical Engineering (BEng) from the National University of Singapore. He is also a Professional Engineer (P Eng, Singapore), Chartered Engineer (C Eng, UK) and Fellow Member of several prestigious professional institutes, namely Chartered Institute of Marketing (FCIM), Chartered Management Institute (FCMI), Institute of Mechanical Engineers (FIMechE), Marketing Institute of Singapore (FMIS), Institute of Electrical Engineers (FIEE) and Senior Member of Singapore Computer Society (SMSCS). He is also a Practising Management Consultant (PMC) certified by the Singapore government.

PREFACE

The first decade of the new millennium has ended. The first decade started with the global economy booming and ended with the world in a recession and signs of recovery still weak. The patient fortunately has survived thanks to some surgeries and medication in the form of fiscal stimulus given by various governments around the world. While some economies, notably China and India, are recovering faster than the others the overall situation continues to be one of a weak recovery. This brings fresh challenges to many companies in Asia and around the world. As these companies venture into the new era, many will fail as they are unable to cope with the rapid pace of changes in the turbulent business environment. This inability may be due to antiquated strategies, obsolete products, poor management, corporate arrogance and many other factors that will be discussed in the modules of this toolkit. Conventional wisdom and business practices that worked in the past might not work in the future and companies are thrown into a state of disarray and chaos. Past successes will not guarantee future successes.

The Asian economic miracle was invincible in the 1990s and would have heralded the 21st century as the Asian century. Unfortunately, this promising scenario ended abruptly in 1997. The economic crisis which started in Thailand quickly escalated and triggered massive capital outflows from Malaysia, Indonesia, South Korea and other parts of Southeast Asia. This sent shock waves that were felt not only in Asia, but also in the stock markets of Latin America (most notably Brazil, Argentina and Mexico). These financial and asset price crises also set the stage for large currency depreciations. Not only the currencies of Thailand, the Philippines, Malaysia, Indonesia and Singapore were affected, but those of South Korea and Taiwan also suffered. Eventually, these sudden events precipitated in the Asian currency meltdown. Barely following the economic crisis of 1997, many companies in Asia are now being overwhelmed by macro factors such as worldwide recession brought forth by the economic recessions in the United States and Japan as well as political turmoil and regional economic malaise. Others have been swept off their feet by micro factors such as market liberalization, proliferation of mergers and acquisitions, emergence of China as a formidable competitor, escalating costs and a host of other factors.

Good managers always conduct a post-mortem to find out what has gone awry, not so much to apportion blame, but to ensure that the same problems do not surface again. The recent economic downturn of 2008 has left a situation of global financial chaos. During September 2008, the crisis hit its most critical stage. There was the equivalent of a bank run on money market mutual funds, which frequently invest in commercial paper issued by corporations to fund their operations and payrolls. Withdrawal from money markets was $144.5 billion during one week, versus $7.1 billion the week prior. This interrupted the ability of corporations to rollover their short-term debt. The U.S. government responded by extending insurance for money market accounts analogous to bank deposit insurance via a temporary guarantee and with Federal Reserve Programs to purchase commercial paper. However, even chaos has its patterns. The post-mortem is the process of ascertaining the patterns of things that have gone wrong so that these mistakes will not be repeated in the future.

In 2010, banks all over the world remained reluctant to lend money to each other or to other borrowers, and the total amount of money loaned to private firms in developed economies would definitely decrease in 2010.

For the re-capitalization of banks by their governments, the banking systems in the United States would possibly require 275 billion to 500 billion dollars, according to estimates made by the IMF's "Global Financial Stability Report", and the banking systems in the whole of Europe (excluding Britain) would require 475 billion to 950 billion dollars, and the banking systems in Britain would need 125 billion to 250 billion dollars.

In the past, it was "three strikes and you were out." Today, one strike and you are history. This is because today's world is highly competitive and you may not have a second chance. Through one mistake, miscalculation or strategic error, your competitors can steal your customers very quickly. Your margins for errors are very thin as resources are scarce. This amplifies the importance of post-mortem to minimise repeating the mistakes. This principle applies strongly to the current credit crisis still affecting the world in 2010-11.

To avoid being a victim of the current economic depression, companies must know the market and stay ahead of the curve. This is what has kept Google from falling by the wayside. Because they have continued to foster innovation and have taken conservative risks in their business model, they continued to prosper in 2010 – a rare thing in the current economy. This also clearly shows the power of the Internet. This evolving medium is by no means insulated from the normal economy. That Google has managed to continue to grow in the face of an economic crisis speaks well of the company, and also of the Internet.

In this rapidly evolving and exciting scenario many companies that are healthy will prosper while others will need support. Some will become chronically ill and die (bankrupt like Lehman Brothers), while others will need surgery and therapy. This toolkit is designed to help you make your company healthy and keep it that way.

2010' Corporate Turnaround Centre

WELCOME TO THE TRANSFORMATION TOOLKIT

Objectives of the Transformation Toolkit

At the end of this Toolkit, it is expected that you will be able to diagnose a potential case of corporate illness, devise a well-defined set of steps that need to be undertaken to treat the entity and bring it back to better health in the short run as well as in the long run. In this context, this Toolkit is designed to help you through this process. The specific objectives of the Toolkit are:

- To provide a complete guide to the author's approach to Corporate Turnaround.
- The broad structure is derived from the book *"Corporate Turnaround: Nursing a Sick Company Back to Health."*
- Key concepts and issues that have been integrated from the author's other books are: *"Corporate Wellness"*, *"Ultimate Internet Marketing Strategies and Tactics"*, *"Corporate Turnaround and Transformation Methodology"*, *"What We Can Learn From the Animals About Office Politics"*, *"Turnaround Yourself"* and *"Inspirational Notebook"*
- Through a series of exercises, to enable you to apply Corporate Turnaround principles to your own situation.
- To serve as a reference document for any future help that you might require.

Description of the Transformation Toolkit

The principles of Corporate Turnaround rely extensively on the medical analogy espoused by the author. This Toolkit adopts a logical and user-friendly approach in bringing out the processes involved in Corporate Turnaround and is

2010 ' Corporate Turnaround Centre

designed for use as a study guide to accompany the book, *Corporate Turnaround: Nursing a Sick Company Back to Health* by Dr. Mike Teng. Throughout the Toolkit, exercises and opportunities are provided for personal reflection and research of the participant's corporation or organization so that the learning is specific to your needs.

Modules are arranged in a logical order, which allows you to:

- Understand the concept of corporate illness and its typical symptoms.
- Define the role of each of the three phases of treatment: Surgery, Resuscitation, and Therapy.
- Plan and execute the steps involved in each phase of treatment within the context of your organization to facilitate a holistic recovery in a turnaround situation.

~

"Corporate Turnaround"

If these troubled times – Find you in a bind.
Stuck at a mountain – Too steep to climb.
When you're going down – Reach out for our hand,
We can salvage the pieces – We can make a plan.

One step at a time – Always gaining ground,
We can make it happen – Corporate Turnaround.

Don't sit and worry – And don't just sit and stare,
The sooner we get started – The quicker we'll get there.
We can take the problem – Turn it into gold,
We can help you make it – Before you lose control.

One step at a time – Always gaining ground,
We can make it happen – Corporate Turnaround.

You don't have to be down – Or on the way to distress,
When you're doing fine – That's the time to address
Before it gets too late – Before it starts to slide,
Let us show you how – To keep on top of the ride.

One step at a time – Always gaining ground,
We can make it happen – Corporate Turnaround

2010´ Corporate Turnaround Centre

WHAT IS CORPORATE TURNAROUND?

With early intervention, many potential 'corporate failures' can actually be nursed back to robust health, using the proven and tested corporate turnaround techniques discussed in this resource. Thus, this Toolkit is an invaluable tool for corporate turnaround CEOs and Managers to rescue ailing companies. Many successful companies have been built or rebuilt out of ashes. This Toolkit can help you to do so too. Companies which may not technically fall into the turnaround category but are plagued with situations such as lethargic growth, loss of customers, declining or damaged market influence, high staff attrition, or similar problems, may also find this resource helpful in devising salvation plans. Even for relatively healthy companies with good profitability that are not in the perilous turnaround stage, the steps and practices documented in this resource will serve to strengthen and fortify their companies' performance for sustained long-term growth. One of the messages embodied here is "one does not need to fall sick in order to get well."

Just as it is difficult to provide a precise definition of a turnaround situation, it is also difficult to define what is meant by a complete or holistic recovery. Complete or holistic recovery here means that the company has fully recovered from its cash and profit crisis situation and is now able to sustain recovery and growth in the long term. Therefore, it is unlikely to falter at handling another crisis in the foreseeable future and should be able to embrace the changes in the environment confidently. Once it has achieved complete or holistic recovery, the company will be able to develop sustainable long-term competitive advantage. The implementation of the turnaround process will be illustrated through real-life encounters, as well as some of the best of Eastern and Western practices. The unique usage of medical analogy between the corporation and the human body provides a strong tool for the reader to grasp and understand the complicated subject of corporate failure and turnaround. The exposition of the paramount significance of *qi* or internal energy and

2010 ' Corporate Turnaround Centre

strong immune system as determinants in the corporate well-being are profound, providing the reader with a vivid picture of these dynamic truths.

It is unfortunate that business schools today rarely teach the subject of corporate turnaround. It is a myth that textbook knowledge will suffice in helping these executives manage a corporate turnaround situation which is much more esoteric and complicated. Turnaround executives have to be benevolent dictators, crisis managers, visionaries, entrepreneurs, coaches and spiritual leaders all rolled into one. With so many hats to wear, a turnaround executive may appear schizophrenic exhibiting multiple and at times mutually contradictory qualities. In some tough turnaround situations, the turnaround executives may even need to possess supernatural skills such as the ability to sell a stethoscope to a tree surgeon or to resurrect the dead. As a result, business schools are often relegated to producing textbook executives who are unable to cope with the realities in the marketplace where many sick and troubled companies abound.

There is also an unfortunate belief that the primary role of a turnaround leader is merely to be ruthless and fire people in order to reduce costs. This turnaround model book attempts to alert and prevent companies from reaching the terminal stage when all treatments are in vain. It also serves to illustrate that even a successful company is vulnerable to financial failures. Hence the awareness of the potency of various types of corporate viruses is important. As the saying goes, "Half the cure is found if you are able to identify the disease and what afflicts you." Successful corporate turnaround should be holistic and based on addressing both strategic and operational issues in the short and long term. Comprehensive turnaround plans should seek not only to cut costs but to grow revenues and change the corporate culture in order to facilitate management of the vagaries of the marketplace in the future. The turnaround management must get a good handle on both the soft "heart" and hard "brain" issues in the organization.

2010 ' Corporate Turnaround Centre

For a holistic and complete corporate recovery, the following three-phased approach (with the medical analogy) is used:

- Phase I Treatment: **Surgery** – To re-structure the troubled organization to face the harsh reality and improve cash flow
- Phase II Treatment: **Resuscitation** – To re-vitalize the business so as to improve the sales revenues and profits
- Phase III Treatment: **Therapy** – To re-habilitate a strong and healthy corporate immune system in order to sustain long-term growth

Many books on corporate turnaround merely stop treatment at Phase I: Corporate Surgery. However, Phase I is not exhaustive enough, as a patient could still die even though the surgery went well. In Phase I, cash flow is of paramount concern. As you move into Phase II, profitability takes on more importance as it is only through profits that one can ensure positive cash flow in the future. Some books may feature a few Phase II resuscitation strategies to build up the sales. The model presented in this approach is one of the few that offers a comprehensive corporate turnaround process to include Phase III: Therapy (Nursing) which deals with the soft issues. Bain & Co. completed an eight-year study of 25,000 public companies; it was published in 1997. To produce one year of good financial results is within the reach of most companies. In any given year, 40 percent of these 25,000 companies grew sales faster than the gross national product (GNP) and profit faster than sales. But it is a rare exception to continue chalking up profitable growth in subsequent years and 94 percent of the same companies failed to do so. The key is to sustain profitable growth. This is why the third phase, therapy, is crucial for successful completion of the entire corporate turnaround process and ensuring a clean bill of health.

The third phase involves a change in the corporate culture, without which restructuring is similar to upgrading a cancer-stricken patient to a more expensive ward in the hospital. It only treats the symptoms and not the root cause of the ailment. Rapid changes in the environment are causing the quick demise of once successful companies. The mandate for change is not coming; it has arrived with a vengeance. The effective response to deal with these rapid changes is to build a strong and healthy corporate culture that resembles the strong immune system of a body that can fight against the ravages brought about by some of these changes. This book expounds the ways to strengthen the corporate immune system by eating a balanced diet through vision, feedback and action, promoting active communication, cultivating a positive mental attitude and emphasizing exercise which is training and development. A new and better approach to office politics is also prescribed for this phase. A strong immune system embraces the mandala concept of a new corporate philosophy and free flow of internal energy, *qi*. It also engenders the management mantra of action orientation which is being flexible, fast and innovative so that the organization can respond rapidly to changes. Corporate turnaround is a near-death experience whereas corporate transformation is a revival experience.

"Corporate Transformation"

Your company is like a person, full of life and soul
Looking after its health, should be your goal
We can help you, in these uncertain times.
Or if you are flying, we'll make sure you won't decline.

Chorus
Corporate transformation is the only way
Corporate transformation will save the day
Tried and tested means that pave the way
So if you're flying high, we'll keep you in the sky

If you're getting itchy about growth and profits

If it's looking sticky and it feels like you've lost it
If you feel it could be better, then it probably can
We have respected methods from an expert hand

Tycoons and academics have all agreed
That the three-phase plan is the way to succeed,
Surgery, resuscitation, and therapy
Will keep your company where it should be

Chorus
Corporate transformation is the only way
Corporate transformation will save the day
Tried and tested means that pave the way
So if you're flying high, we'll keep you in the sky

You want to keep the competition at arm's length,
If you use our know how and strategies, it will all make sense,
And your company will carry on, and profit will not run dry
Your shareholders will be so happy, they'll start to cry

Don't be afraid of restructure, it's part of the game,
Don't be lacklustre when it comes to change,
Don't blink or hesitate when you have the chance,
To revitalise or innovate, as it gives a positive stance.

Chorus
Corporate transformation is the only way
Corporate transformation will save the day
Tried and tested means that pave the way
So if you're flying high, we'll keep you in the sky

MODULE #1

–

DIAGNOSIS

–

IDENTIFY THE

BOTTLENECKS

PHYSICAL AND FISCAL HEALTH – THE MEDICAL ANALOGY

Human Being versus Company

There is a strong parallel between corporations and medical science. In fact, a company can fall sick just like a human being. Contrary to the common view, a company is not an inanimate object; it is a community of people, a living organism and an entity with its own distinct personality and attitudes. Therefore, without proper care, a company which has life of its own, will also perish.

The table below illustrates some of the comparative analogies between the human being and the company from antenatal to birth to living and death. At the antenatal stage, just as in the case of the impregnation of the human embryo, a company is formed through a concept wherein the founder explores or brainstorms the initial idea. In the case of the person, the foetus will be nurtured through antenatal care till birth. For the company, the concept will germinate into a feasibility report on its viability, followed by gestation and preparation, culminating in its start-up. At birth, the start-up company is a baby. Some babies are stillborn and aborted due to various viral attacks which will be described later.

Human Being	The Company
Pregnancy	Concept/Idea
Baby	Start-up Company
Healthy	Good Profitability and Cash Flow
Marriage	Merger and Acquisition
Patient	Troubled Company
Sickness/Ailment/Disease	Trouble/Problem

2010 ' Corporate Turnaround Centre

Lifeblood	Cash flow
Haemorrhage	Loss of Key Staff
Viral Attacks	Internal and External Negative Factors that Affect the Company
Tumours/Cancers	Dysfunctional Employees
Doctor	Turnaround CEO/Manager
Hospital	Bank/Private Investor/Venture Capitalist
Surgery	Re-structuring/Rationalizing/Downsizing/Re-engineering
Resuscitation	Re-vitalization of Sales and Profits
Therapy	Sustaining/Nurturing Growth; especially of Corporate Culture
Healed	Turned Around
Death	Bankruptcy/Close-Down/Wound Up
Undertaker	Liquidator
Heart	Mindset/Attitude
Heart Attack/Stroke	Major Business Failure/Strategic Error
Culture	Corporate Culture/Immune System
Internal Energy/Qi	Drive/Passion
DNA	Business Model
Biological Nervous System	Digital Nervous System

A healthy and living person is like a profitable company, full of vitality (expanding) and energy (contributing) whereas a patient or sick person is akin to a company plagued by problems. The trouble, sickness, ailment or disease in the case of the company is usually financial but can be manifested in other forms as highlighted later in this chapter. The company is as vulnerable to viral attacks as the human being. These are manifested as internal and external negative factors impinging on its health. The company's cash flow is equivalent to the lifeblood of the human being and it can encounter losses or negative cash flow, similar to a human being afflicted with haemorrhage. In some cases,

2010' Corporate Turnaround Centre

the company is adversely affected by dysfunctional employees, much like the case of uncontrolled growth of tumours or cancers within the human anatomy.

The doctor for the company is the turnaround CEO or Manager who brings healing or resuscitation to a sick company, accomplishing a turnaround. The hospital is the bank, private investor or venture capitalist that provides the vital financing and cash flow for the troubled company to sustain itself. The surgery is known by a host of corporate euphemisms such as re-structuring, rationalizing, downsizing, and re-engineering. They all mean the same thing. If you have been a casualty of re-engineering, it basically means that you have been fired. When a company falls sick with a major disease, it needs to undergo surgery and intensive care treatments in order to recover and heal itself. The intensive care treatments are the turnaround techniques used to resuscitate the company back to health. When the company is healed, it is successfully turned around, otherwise death in the form of financial collapse or bankruptcy ensues. In the case of the company, the undertaker is the liquidator spelling its demise or death.

The nursing of the company requires a change of mindset and attitude (heart) and corporate culture (culture). Medical science has generally found that in psychosomatic ailments, a person's mental attitude, mindset, psyche and anxiety can have tremendous impact on his or her physical health. In some cases, this can result in paranoia. In others, the inability to cope with stress can cause heart problems such as strokes, heart attacks and even cancer. Similarly in a company, the wrong and negative attitudes of the staff can create a dysfunctional corporate culture. The corporate culture is like the immune system of a company. The equivalent concept of internal energy or *qi* (as used in Chinese medicine) or *reiki* (the Japanese equivalent) in the human person can be broadly translated as the drive and passion that are the hallmarks of many successful and excellent companies. The company's business models are the basic "building blocks", equivalent to the human deoxyribonucleic acid (DNA). For example, many dot.com companies need to change their DNA urgently in order to survive as they do not have viable business models to perpetuate. Digital Nervous System is the equivalent of the Biological Nervous System that helps a company to be sensitive to changes in its environment.

If a company is sick, it must quickly seek a proper diagnosis. The correct prognosis may be established after extensive tests (analyses). Thereafter, the healing process can be established through the prescription of the appropriate treatment and correct medication.

When dealing with human beings, sicknesses and ill health are usually clearly visible and quickly diagnosed. For example, a sick person down with flu may manifest symptoms of cough, running nose, fever and body aches. The doctor is able to determine the magnitude of the fever by using a thermometer.

It is the same with the company. Usually there are ample warning signs or symptoms of impending trouble. However, these warning signals are often ignored or suppressed; hence the onset of a crisis comes as a surprise. It is tragic that many companies fail, not due solely to the irrevocable downward spiral of their financial health, but because of management's inability or unwillingness to face these serious problems squarely and take appropriate timely action. The management may be in a state of self-denial or does not wish to let others know about the company's predicament. Such denial is insidious, resulting in delays in the implementation of vital remedial actions during the early stages of under-performance. Prompt action on the other hand could dramatically improve the company's chances of survival and secure its resurrection or rejuvenation. Sometimes top executives fall into the denial trap as acknowledging the problem is tantamount to admission of failure, exposing them to criticism by the company's board of directors, shareholders and peers within the larger corporate structures.

Many companies have annual medical examinations and health screenings for

2010 ' Corporate Turnaround Centre

their employees but are negligent when it comes to their own check-ups. Poor management and financial information systems typically get blamed for management's inability to "see it coming". However, the traditional accounting methods such as balance sheets and profit and loss statements only capture the measurable financial aspects of the company at a certain point in time. There may be many non-quantifiable factors that may impinge upon the health of the company.

By the time the sickness is clearly manifested in the company accounts, it may already be too late to take corrective actions to reverse the situation. It is therefore difficult to assess the reasons for the decline and failure of companies because early diagnosis is not possible. Let's look more closely at these financial tools.

2010 ' Corporate Turnaround Centre

FAILINGS OF TRADITIONAL FINANCIAL MEASUREMENTS

Most companies use traditional financial measurements to track their fiscal well-being. Staying with the medical analogy, this is like checking your temperature but neglecting your blood pressure. We usually recognize feeling feverish, and use a thermometer to confirm the feeling. High blood pressure is an important early warning, but we do not "feel" this condition.

Likewise, financial measurements do not provide the earliest warnings. Financial problems are the result of a deeper condition. Corrective action can only be taken after a problem is noticed. The sooner this happens, the better

Investors may use the figures from the company's annual report to calculate ratios and decide whether to buy or sell shares. If the financial conditions have already worsened, then the investment community will respond. This does not benefit the company.

What diagnostic tools should have been used to detect the causes of these problems?

Several Traditional Financial Measurements

Here is a sample of traditional financial measurements:

- **Growth and Profitability**:
    - Growth = (This year's turnover minus last year's turnover) / (Last year's turnover), as a percentage
    - Profitability = (Operating profit) / Turnover, as a percentage

2010 ' Corporate Turnaround Centre

- **Cash**:
  - Current Ratio = (Current Assets) / (Current Liabilities)
  - Quick Ratio = (Current Assets minus Stocks) / (Current Liabilities)
  - Debt Collection Period = (Trade Debtors times 365) / Turnover
  - Trade Credit Period = (Trade Creditors times 365) / (Cost of Sales, raw materials and consumables)
  - Stock Turnover = (Cost of Sales) / (Closing Stock)
- **Investment**:
  - Net Capital Investment versus sales = (Net Book Value of tangible fixed assets) / Turnover, as a percentage
  - Average Age of tangible fixed assets = (Accumulated Depreciation) / Cost of Assets, as a percentage
- **Financing**:
  - Gearing Ratio = Debt / (Debt plus Equity), as a percentage
  - Effective Interest Rate on borrowing = (Interest Payback) / (Average of opening and closing debt), as a percentage
  - Dividend Cover = (Profit for the fiscal year) / Dividends

Non-Financial Measurements

What, then, are some non-financial diagnostic measurements for the corporation? These are discussed in more detail in the "**Corporate Viruses – Internal**" section. Briefly, these identify problem areas inside an organization. Use "**Exercise 1.2**" several times, perhaps on a monthly or quarterly basis, and then assess whether your company is running a fever.

WHY DO COMPANIES FAIL?

The most obvious warning signs of impending business failures may include the following:

- Negative/declining profitability
- Deteriorating market position
- Poor or negative cash position, with an inability to satisfy its cash obligations
- High staff turnover or low morale

The profitability barometer of a vulnerable company usually takes the form of negative or declining profitability. Furthermore, profits may be persistently low and have been slipping unabated for the past few years. Any profit is often consistently below the industry's average and compares unfavourably with competitors selling similar products/services. This poor performance in profit is a telling sign of corporate ailment, similar to a person having a fever, warning that the body is not well.

Deteriorating market position can be seen through the loss in the company's market share, a drop in the number of its key distributors or dealers, or margin erosion of its products. Oftentimes, low-cost competitors are nibbling at the company's market share for some time without the company even realizing it. When the company finally wakes up, it is shocked to discover that some of its major customers or key markets have been taken away.

When this occurs, rapid deterioration in its liquidity sets in and it is unable to make ends meet. The cash-strapped company is constantly juggling its cash resources to satisfy the most pressing cash obligations. Such frequent cash crunches can pose severe strains on the company's already over-stretched working capital. The problem may be further compounded by reduced availability of existing bank lines. The financial institutions offering such

2010 ' Corporate Turnaround Centre

facilities start to tighten credit when they become aware of the company's financial woes. More serious cases involve defaulting bond interest payments/repayments, loan instalments, etc., which can rapidly degenerate into hopeless scenarios of bankruptcies.

Troubled companies' ailing health is often exacerbated by high staff turnover (particularly loss of top-management personnel) and low morale. These can stem from many factors including mismanagement and poor prospects.

The warning signs of impending corporate failures are perhaps the cumulative effects of many underlying or root causes. Among the many possible causes, the most significant one is undoubtedly the quality of the CEO. Most turnaround situations arise because of the CEO's incompetence, ineffectiveness, carelessness, ego and/or inexperience. It is simply too much to ask or expect incumbent management to be objective in evaluating its past performance when they are the same people who by mismanagement, allowed the firm's financial health to deteriorate in the first place.

A "Trend Watch" survey by the Turnaround Management Association completed in February 2003 also concurred with the PriceWaterhouseCoopers' findings. It was revealed that poor management, in the opinion of most respondents (58%) was the primary reason for any company's under-performance across all industries. Other factors mentioned included over-leveraging (37%); faulty business models (30%) and increased competition (22%).

The troubled company usually manifests two types of problems, internal and external, which will be discussed as internal and external viruses in our medical analogy. The key is to identify these viruses and eliminate them, as well as to fortify your company's immune system to combat them before they can enter and inflict major damage to your company's system. This is akin to prophylaxis (treatment for preventing diseases); prevention is better than cure.

EXERCISE 1.1
YOUR COMPANY'S BROADER CONTEXT

Use the **PESTLE** analysis tool to consider the broader issues that you will need to take into account when looking at Corporate Turnaround.

Political - *Consider factors such as tax policies, environmental regulations, trade restrictions, tariffs, political stability, etc.*	**E**conomic - *Consider the impact of economic growth or recession, interest rates, exchange rates, and the rate of inflation.*
Social - *Consider cultural issues such as health awareness, population growth rate, age distribution, career attitudes, etc.*	**T**echnological - *Consider automation, technological incentives, rate of technology change; impact of the Internet, etc.*
Legal - *Consider employment/labour law, discrimination law, consumer law, health & safety law, etc.*	**E**nvironmental - *Consider weather, climate, climate change, green issues, recycling, etc.*

2010 ' Corporate Turnaround Centre

This analysis tool gives you a picture of the factors that are influencing your strategic management and decision-making and will give you an idea of the broader, global context in which you will be applying the Corporate Turnaround methodology. Next, let's take a closer look at the differences between internal and external conditions, starting with "internal viruses"

2010 ' Corporate Turnaround Centre

CORPORATE VIRUSES – INTERNAL

A virus is a simple micro-organism that is parasitic and disease-causing. Since a company is just as vulnerable to viral attacks as a human being, it is imperative for it to identify (diagnose) any potential viral infection and seek the relevant preventive measures or remedies (i.e. appropriate medication or treatment) as early as possible before its health deteriorates. But the human body does not produce pathogens (organisms causing disease), such as internal viruses. Once a virus enters the human body, it will infect it and then use the human cells to replicate or reproduce its own species. The closest equivalent to an internal virus is probably the group of ailments known as autoimmune diseases. A person has an autoimmune disease when his immune system mistakenly attacks the organs, cells and tissues of his own body. One of the most common autoimmune diseases is rheumatoid arthritis where the antibodies of the body attack the tissue lining of joints of the body causing inflammation and thickening of these tissues, thus disabling the patient and causing death in some cases. Other examples of autoimmune diseases are lupus, multiple sclerosis, myasthenia gravis and inflammatory bowel disease.

Besides being susceptible to external viruses, corporations can generate their own internal viruses. Internal viruses refer mainly to factors that are more *micro* in nature and often emanate from the organization. On the other hand, external viruses are *macro* in nature and usually not within the company's control. Some examples of these are shown in the table below:

Internal	External
Management problems • Arrogance • Procrastination • Incompetent CEOs/Managers • Resistance to change • Poor quality staff • Lapses in internal control	• Government intervention/regulations • Economic recession • Political turmoil • Low-cost competitors • Appreciating/depreciating currencies • Changes in consumer behaviour • Environmental/health issues

2010 ' Corporate Turnaround Centre

Bad financial control	Technological changes
• Cash flow • Accounting System • Budgetary control	• Natural disasters • Shortage of workers/raw materials • Labour unrest • Terrorist attacks
Operational weaknesses	
• High costs • Weak logistics • Bad marketing	
Human resource problems	
• Negative Attitudes • High staff turnover • Other factors	
Major project fiasco	
• Over-leveraging	

Internal Viral Attacks

Many internal viruses are generated by the company and are actually within the company's control. They are usually associated with weak management and a poor financial system. Some internal viruses are caused by genetic defects and DNA such as dysfunctional corporate culture of the past. The onslaught of this form of viral attack can lead to bad or untimely business decisions, poor financial control and other related problems. The following review of some of these internal viral attacks, though not exhaustive, provides us with a snapshot of the severity of these infections. They can inflict deadly damage and seriously hamper the company's health and chances of recovery once the harm has been done.

Management Problems

According to the surveys cited earlier, this is the single biggest factor behind many business failures. Management can pose many serious forms of "viral attacks" such as:

- **Arrogance** resulting from corporate success and/or deliberate self-denial or refusal to acknowledge salient changes that are taking place in the market environment, competition, etc. This can result in failure to plan for the overall strategy, or misjudgement in reading the marketplace. A sense of superiority sometimes permeates the whole corporate culture.

- **Procrastination** can strike a company in a very subtle manner. It could get stuck and operate in the realm of inactivity or *status quo* as no one at the top echelon wants to make important business decisions. This could be due to management's indecision or fear of failure. In the medical analogy, it is akin to a stroke victim or a person stricken in a coma.

- **Incompetent CEOs or Managers** can arise from the hiring of the wrong people, those who may lack the necessary expertise and skills or they simply do not possess the necessary business acumen for the company's operations. This can result in poor or untimely decisions and can diminish the company's opportunities for growth and expansion in the ever-changing world of business. This type of virus can literally snuff out the company's life, causing corporate asphyxia or suffocation.

~

Sun Tzu's *"Art of War"* has been treasured and passed down for 2,500 years. Sun Tzu (544–496 BC) wrote the original text shortly before 510 BC. The text was preserved in China and brought to the West by the French. Napoleon used its strategy to conquer Europe. Sun Tzu had a dramatic effect on Chinese history. After his hiring by the king, the kingdom of Wu emerged to become the most powerful state of the period. Sun Tzu acknowledged the critical role played by CEOs (Generals) when he said: "When the General is weak and without authority, when his orders are not clear and distinct, when there are no fixed duties assigned to officers and men and when the ranks are formed in a slovenly haphazard manner, the result is utter disorganization."

~

- **Resistance to change** can be caused by tradition or stereotyping resulting in constraints such as the company being forced to fit into a "mould"[1] syndrome. Unfortunately this mould may be outdated or irrelevant. Any new ideas or sparks of creativity will be dismissed as

---

[1] American spelling: ⬜mold⬜

2010 ' Corporate Turnaround Centre

unconventional, radical or simply not feasible. This often results in the company missing excellent opportunities for breakthroughs.

- **Poor-quality staff** can also sabotage the company's operations. Unlike the case of incompetent CEOs/managers who fail to provide direction for the company, staffing of poor-quality executives can derail the implementation of the company's goals and strategies. In addition, badly trained staff or misfits can adversely affect the company's business and image. These may be manifested in poor customer service, declining sales and shrinking market share.

- **Lapses in internal control** due to the Management's disregard for internal control or weak control can cause serious damage, usually financial in nature. This can range from failure to report errors, to thefts and even fraud. In some instances, serious lapses can result in revocation of business licenses and even collapse of the entire company.

Bad Financial Control

This encompasses numerous aspects and may include the following:

- **Cash flow** problems arise from poor cash management. Even companies with good products or services can literally be "choked" to death by poor cash flow as they are unable to continue with the normal daily operations.

- **Accounting systems** are critical to the company's financial health, as they have tremendous impact on its profitability and long-term viability. Efficient monitoring of pricing, margins, costs, etc., is vital, since rapid deterioration, especially in liquidity position, can set in if such areas are neglected. This is somewhat similar to a person's need for constant monitoring of his blood pressure and cholesterol levels if he wishes to avoid any possibility of a future heart attack.

- **Budgetary control** cannot be over-emphasized as the close monitoring of all relevant expenses and income streams are vital. Poor budgetary control can result in improper allocation of resources and inability to

2010 ' Corporate Turnaround Centre

foresee problems that require immediate attention.

Careful surveillance, on the other hand, allows the company to anticipate possible problem areas, thereby enabling it to take timely and appropriate corrective measures to prevent or rectify the situation. This is similar to the case of a health-conscious person who is constantly monitoring his weight, diet, activity levels and other relevant details in order to prevent the onset of ailments or complications relating to obesity and heart diseases.

Operational Weaknesses

Through vigilance, a company can ward off major viral attacks manifested in the form of high costs, product obsolescence, poor marketing, logistics/production problems and other operational factors. As some of these attacks are often swift, the company can be left crippled and even face its demise within a short time span if it is unable to administer the antidote quickly. Many examples are cited in later chapters of this book.

Human Resource Problems

Human resource problems are often the causes of failures of companies and these include the following:

- **Negative attitudes and mindsets** of the staff may be so entrenched within the corporation that it is literally the case of fighting the enemy within – "We are our own enemies." Negative attitudes can spread like wildfire and show up in various forms such as low morale, low productivity, high staff turnover, etc. If left unaddressed, they can have lingering and serious repercussion on the company's competitive edge, customer service and, of course, its bottom line. This is much like the case of allergy or diarrhea when the allergens or toxins are not eliminated from the human body.

2010 ' Corporate Turnaround Centre

- **High staff turnover** is costly and the defection of key personnel to competitors will further hinder the company's ability to compete in the marketplace. Sometimes, the underlying problem lies in the company's inability to develop and motivate its employees. This is usually due to poor training, resulting in employees who are resistant to change and lagging behind the competition.

- **Other factors** include poor employee-retention incentive programs. Not all incentive plans will work. Some of these plans encourage staff to maintain the *status quo* while others provoke employees to manipulate results (through "creative" accounting or other unethical practices such as manipulation of stock prices) so that the company appears to be doing well when, in fact, it is not so.

Major Project Fiasco

This could result from a host of factors, including poor project management, inaccurate costing/pricing, budget overrun, etc. Consequently, the company is unable to complete the project within the contracted timeframe. This can lead to legal ramifications, such as compensation in liquidated damages, forfeiture of tender bonds, as well as detrimental consequences of tarnished reputation and poor track records. The latter can severely limit the company's future earnings prospects.

- **Over-leveraging** – A company may over-trade or expand too quickly into non-core business areas, geographical regions or unfamiliar areas. One of the most common internal problems relating to bankruptcy is excessive leveraging of the company's assets. The company is trying to do too much with too little. Hence, it is particularly vulnerable if it is hit unexpectedly by events such as currency depreciation, a sudden rise in interest rates or if the bankers withdraw their credit facilities. Consequently, there are severe strains on existing financial, manpower and other resources.

2010' Corporate Turnaround Centre

A too-rapid expansion coupled with under-capitalisation can be deadly Diversification efforts may have become too broad and the company is spreading itself too thin. Concentration and building of strong positions in fewer businesses may be the key to improving your long-term financial performance. For survival, the company must source for additional funding. However, this is a vicious cycle, as with its weak financial position, the distressed company may incur higher interests and fees in sourcing for its funds, thereby further weakening its profitability and cash flow.

Treatment for Internal Viruses

Most of these internal viruses are perpetuated by a poor or incompetent management team and CEO. An example of the importance of having a good CEO is illustrated through Ansett, Australia's number two domestic carrier. Ansett Australia was suffering from financial woes and unable to find a financial saviour. It was haemorrhaging at A$1 million a week, with its debts estimated at more than A$2 billion (US$1 billion). Its founder, Reginald Ansett, grew the airline from modest beginnings in 1936. Sir Reginald, who was knighted for the success of Ansett, was the driving force behind Ansett's rise. In 1979, non-airline industry players, Rupert Murdoch's News Ltd and transport company TNT bought the Ansett airline and pushed Sir Reginald into a figurehead position until his death in 1981.

The absence of Sir Reginald left the airline without a strong leader. The new owners were not in the industry for the long term and made several bad decisions about its plane fleet and also implemented detrimental cost-cutting exercises to trim the operations in preparation for a profitable sale. Air New Zealand bought a 50 percent stake from TNT in 1996 but it was too late to save Ansett. The problems were further compounded in 2001 by a series of embarrassing maintenance oversights that led to the grounding of its entire fleet of aging Boeing 767s, further eroding public confidence in the airline. Ansett was subsequently overwhelmed by the internal viral attack of poor

2010 ' Corporate Turnaround Centre

management. The loss of the strong CEO, Sir Reginald, coupled with the incompetence of his successors caused the downfall of Ansett. The post-9/11 problems proved the final nail in the coffin and Ansett ceased operations on 4th March 2002 and is now under liquidation and administration.

Another example of a bad CEO is illustrated by Henry McKinnell, Pfizer's CEO from 2001-2006. McKinnell took the company in a disastrous acquisition direction where it overpaid for companies and securities that added nothing to its drug pipeline - Pfizer's core business. Yet, when he walked away after losing billions of shareholder dollars, he took an additional $213 million as a retirement package that included an $82 million pension, stock and other benefits. Pfizer lost more than $137 billion in market value during his tenure.

Sometimes, a blood transfusion or surgery is required to change the whole management team and eliminate the internal viruses. The medical analogy for eliminating internal viruses may merit the use of Western medical treatments such as vaccination or surgery, which calls for a standardised, invasive, scientific and analytical approach. The equivalent of this in the corporate context would be downsizing, restructuring, new market development, etc. The key is that one must administer the medicine quickly before the patient takes a turn for the worse. This is described in Phases I and II of the turnaround process.

2010 ' Corporate Turnaround Centre

EXERCISE 1.2

ASSESSMENT OF INTERNAL VIRUSES

STAGE ONE:

Use the table and 6-point scale below to rate the current impact of the following internal viruses on your company's performance and fiscal health.

INTERNAL VIRUSES	IMPACT					
	None	Low	~	Moderate	~	High
	0	1	2	3	4	5
Management problems						
Arrogance Procrastination Incompetent CEOs/Managers Resistance to change Poor quality staff Lapses in internal control						
Bad financial control						
Cash flow Accounting System Budgetary control						
Operational weaknesses						
High costs Weak logistics Bad marketing						
Human resource problems						
Negative Attitudes High staff turnover Other factors						
Major project fiasco						
Over-leveraging						
TOTAL						

Note that this table has 16 rows ("Arrogance", "Procrastination", etc.), where each row can score from zero to 5. So the whole chart's total score can range from an impossibly perfect zero to the walking death of 90. As a rule, the score

2010' Corporate Turnaround Centre

results in a diagnosis:

- Below 40: Healthy, but do check any one high score
- 40-60: Mild fever, so prioritize and address the issues
- 61-80: Moderate fever, so start moving on several issues
- Over 80: High fever, and immediate remedial action must begin

STAGE TWO:

Now identify the priority issues for action under each internal virus heading.

Management Problems

Bad Financial Control

Operational Weaknesses

Human Resource Problems

Major Project Fiascos

STAGE THREE:

Assess the treatment that you have administered so far to tackle these internal viruses:

What steps have you already taken to improve the performance and fiscal health of your company?

What has been the impact/effectiveness of these actions?

What next steps do you expect to take, and when?

CORPORATE VIRUSES - EXTERNAL

External viruses, being macro in nature are often beyond the company's control. The entire industry or marketplace, or even the whole country, may be stricken by the same type of external virus. The attacks can be silent, swift, and often appear non-threatening at the beginning. But all of them can deal a life-threatening blow to the company, industry or country, or even globally. Owing to the unforeseen and elusive nature of external viral attacks, it is almost impossible to anticipate or pre-empt them, or to estimate the magnitude of ramifications. These external viral attacks can come from the most unexpected quarters.

Even the legendary Jack Welch, who was appointed as the CEO of General Electric in 1981, was inaccurate in two of his external viral predictions. I was a young engineer then working at a General Electric (U.S.) factory based in Singapore and recalled the two predictions made by Welch. He predicted that inflation – then running at 20 percent in the U.S. – would always be a double-digit rate. He also predicted, again wide off the mark, that the Japanese economic juggernaut would soon overtake the U.S. Welch was wrong on both accounts.

Life is full of uncertainties, and so is business.

2010' Corporate Turnaround Centre

Types of External Viruses

Let us examine the typical examples of external viruses depicted in the earlier table.

Government Intervention

Government intervention is like the paradoxical double-edged sword – bringing tremendous business potential for those who are positively affected, but woe to those who are negatively afflicted. Charles Dickens (1812–70), a great English novelist, wrote, "It was the best of times; it was the worst of times." Government intervention in some ways can seriously jeopardise or curtail a company's operations. It may find that the playing field changed literally overnight.

Economic Recession

This virus is of special significance as it can literally drag companies, industries and even the entire economy into the doldrums within a relatively short span of time. Worst still, if this kind of viral attack prevails over a long period of time, many companies will eventually shut down. So deadly is this form of virus that even the hospitals (i.e., banks) in our medical analogy are not immune to it. In an Asia-wide poll, 5 regional experts ranked threats posed by the slowdown in regional economies much higher than political differences, social instability or terrorism. They felt that the economically weak state of the region could do more damage than weak governments or external interference. To quote Roilo Golez, Philippines National Security Adviser from 2001 to 2004, "The economic downturn has a direct effect on the deterioration of peace and internal stability."

2010 ' Corporate Turnaround Centre

Political Turmoil

We are entering a historical era with unprecedented instability since the Cold War. This is characterised by heightened polarisation of ethnic and religious groups resulting in the escalation of widespread anarchy. As mentioned earlier, there is positive correlation between economic conditions and the political situation. Generally, they operate in concert with the achievement of greater political stability during times of economic prosperity. Conversely, times of political turmoil will inevitably lead to social unrest and wreak economic havoc, with the prevalence of events such as riots, looting, military cross-fires and even wars. As confidence crumbles in the midst of political turmoil brewing within a country, or even the entire region or economic bloc, a spiral of events or domino effect often results in the exodus of funds and investments, closure of businesses (initially by large MNCs, then local businesses), high unemployment, etc. Countries like Afghanistan, Somalia, Yemen, Sudan, and Pakistan are examples of how political turmoil can impact economies and operations of companies in their territory.

Low-Cost Competitors

Such a virus can bring forth headaches and even the onset of severe migraines for many companies. This type of attack is acute particularly in companies that pride themselves in the production of highly priced quality products in high fashion and luxury goods such as *haute couture*, exclusive watches, branded handbags and shoes. Each year, substantial portions of their markets are pillaged. The competition does not come only from the proliferation of cheap imitations from third world countries such as China and Thailand, but their businesses are also adversely affected by more cost efficient and productive competitors. The latter are able to produce comparable if not superior quality at a fraction of the price.

2010 ' Corporate Turnaround Centre

The U.S. fruit farmers were stunned by the rocket-like growth in China's apple industry. In order to ward off competition and keep them in business, the U.S. government is giving distressed apple farmers an unprecedented subsidy of US$150 million in market-loss assistance payments. Just within a few short years, China has outstripped the US as the world's largest apple producer. Today, China's apple production exceeds the U.S. by fourfold. Its incredibly low labour costs (in contrast to high U.S. labour costs) have allowed it to keep the prices of its apples down. In the words of one U.S. farmer: "It baffles me how a grower as far away as China can grow, hand-harvest, send his fruit to the processing plant, use all that energy to make apple concentrate, put it in a container, pay a broker, ship it all the way across the ocean, get it hauled and trucked – and still sell it cheaper here (in the U.S.)."[6] Arising from this virus, some U.S. apple farmers are forced out of business while others have switched to alternative crops.

Low-cost competition brings forth a "hollowing-out" effect as companies move to lower-cost production bases in order to reduce costs and boost profitability. Japanese companies have increasingly shifted their production to cheaper countries such as China and Southeast Asia as the average monthly wages in Japan are more than twice those in South Korea and 33 times those in China. According to industry estimates, China now manufactures 40 percent of the world's air-conditioners and 24 percent of its television sets. Nobuo Tanaka, vice president of the Research Institute of Economy, Trade and Industry, a think-tank affiliated with the Trade ministry, reckoned that Japanese imports of China textiles have increased six-fold in the past ten years while its domestic production of fabrics and spun materials has halved. China is becoming the cheap workshop of the world. Even Southeast Asia industries are hollowing out as the multinational companies shift their operations into China. The emergence and proliferation of low-cost competition was later identified as a major killer for many established businesses in the competitive era.

Appreciating/Depreciating Currencies

This virus can strike a company without warning, severely damaging its liquidity position. Viral attacks have also caused the fall of nations. Such a viral attack, though unavoidable at times, may be counteracted by far-sighted measures of the top management through thrift in borrowing and administration of judicious measures, such as currency hedging.

Changes in Consumer Behaviour

Some businesses and industries are particularly vulnerable to this form of viral attack. Fickle and rapid evolution in tastes or trends can render an existing hot-selling item into an instant *passé*. An example in Singapore is that as people become more affluent, they would rather shop at hyper-marts with the full range of products and services, rather than at the neighbourhood provision stores. Also, there is snob appeal in patronizing up-market food and beverage outlets such as Starbucks, The Coffee Bean, and Délifrance, rather than the humble *kopi-tiams* (or coffee shops). Another example is the demise of sewing machines at home, as working women are too busy to do housework, let alone make dresses at home. In addition, as more women join the workforce, there is greater demand for convenience food, TV dinners and pre-mixed sauces, as there is little time to prepare food from scratch.

To stay in business, it is imperative for companies to constantly monitor market trends and update or re-invent themselves. This will allow them ample time to devise appropriate strategies and implement the necessary operational modifications in order to brace themselves for impending elimination from the fiercely competitive marketplace.

Environmental/Health Issues

With increased awareness of conservation, health and other environmental issues, companies that are negatively affected may need to re-invent their products in order to survive. Forward-looking management will be able to rescue their companies from the verge of corporate collapse. An example of such form of attack is the virtual eradication of pig and poultry farming from Singapore arising from pollution and health concerns. Another example is Hilex Poly Co., a South Carolina firm that sells about 30 billion plastic bags annually. They have set up a recycling facility to reprocess bags collected at grocers such as Kroger and A&P stores. The company is selling a bag that will degrade after being exposed to air and sun for several weeks, breaking down into carbon dioxide and water. Also, it is developing technology that measures how many items baggers put in bags to cut down on under-filling. Some of the industry's largest plastic bag producers say they are taking steps to address consumer concerns about their products. Another example is the requirement for the use of CFC[2]-free air-conditioners and refrigerators. Other examples are regulatory requirements on waste disposal and clearance of lands for agricultural use. The Copenhagen Summit that concluded recently has increased pressure on countries to cut emissions of greenhouse gases. Carbon Emissions Trading is already making the polluter companies pay while companies with smaller carbon footprints are earning money. Already some MNCs, like Unilever, have started rating suppliers on their use of sustainable farming techniques.

Technological Changes

This viral attack is also like a double-edged sword, inflicting misfortune on some while being a boon to others. With the rapid technological changes, companies have no alternative but to innovate or risk being eliminated from the highly competitive marketplace. Since the turn of the last century, rapid technological changes resulting in the making of, for example, automobiles, supersonic jets and televisions, have had a profound impact on many

---

[2] Chlorofluorocarbon

2010 ' Corporate Turnaround Centre

industries, redefining and reshaping the rules of the game. The advent of the personal computer (PC) has almost wiped out the need for manual or electric typewriters (except in third world countries) and spelt the demise of companies like Smith Corona. The proliferation of mobile phones and their numerous innovative functions have also rendered pagers obsolete.

The Information Age has redefined and revolutionized the *modus operandi* of many companies across various industries, spearheading developments in computerisation (use of laptops, PCs, etc.), e-commerce, telecommunications (use of mobile phones, facsimile machines, etc.), Internet banking and other state-of-the-art modes of capturing customers. In his book *"The World Is Flat"*, New York Times columnist Thomas Friedman predicts that rugged, adaptable entrepreneurs, equipped with the latest IT infrastructure, will be empowered. The service sector (Telemarketing, Accounting, Computer Programming, Engineering and Scientific research, etc.), will be further outsourced to the English-speaking countries like India. Meanwhile, manufacturing will continue to be off-shored to China.

Natural Disasters

Without warning, a company can be struck by a natural disaster, such as an earthquake, flood or other act of God. Such viral attacks often result in devastating consequences and the afflicted companies could take years to re-establish their businesses in order to regain their pre-disaster stature. Companies need to prepare and expect the unexpected. They should buy fire insurance and have disaster-recovery plans for their computer systems. The Asia tsunami of 2004 resulted in widespread economic losses across the coastal countries in the Indian Ocean region with countries such as Indonesia, Sri Lanka, India, Thailand, Maldives, Malaysia and Bangladesh being impacted. Even African nations such as Kenya and Tanzania suffered damages. Estimates say that the Maldives economy may have been set back by more than 10 years. Another recent example is the earthquake in Haiti. A report by three

Inter-American Development Bank economists found that the Haiti earthquake was more devastating than what the 2004 Indian Ocean tsunami was for Indonesia, and five times deadlier than the 1972 earthquake that levelled Nicaragua's capital. This will cost the nation's economy at least 15 percent of its gross domestic product, as quoted by Pamela Cox, the World Bank's vice president for Latin America and the Caribbean.

Shortage of Workers/Raw Materials

A company's operations can literally come to a standstill if it is unable to resolve problems arising from a shortage of raw materials or workers for its production. The former can give a devastating blow to companies. In 1973, some Middle East Governments cut back on the supply of oil in their conflict with Israel over its occupation of Palestine. This gave rise to the first world oil crisis. A raw materials shortage is especially acute if highly skilled workers are involved. Such a viral attack can be warded off if the company has contingency planning and vigilant logistics and other monitoring systems.

2010 ' Corporate Turnaround Centre

Labour Unrest

Many companies are constantly affected by union unrest and strikes as unions demand higher wages on behalf of employees. For example, the strike by Cathay Pacific's pilots in 2001 cost the company at least HK$350 million (US$45 million), not to mention other intangible losses. The 2009 strike by British Airways staff almost crippled the airline and, if not for the timely intervention by the Government, would have resulted in a crisis. More than 4,000 pilots at Lufthansa airlines launched a four-day strike over pay and job security that grounded two-thirds of the German carrier's flights and cost it $33 million a day. Singapore has solved this problem by banning strikes and fostering a close tripartite relationship amongst the Government, management and labour.

Terrorist Attacks

The terrorist attacks in the U.S. on 11 September 2001 using hijacked commercial aircraft were without precedent in terms of the extensive economic damage and loss of life. The timing could hardly be worse given that fears of a global recession were already rife. Major economic effects arose from the September 11 attacks, with initial shock causing global stock markets to drop sharply. The attacks themselves caused approximately $40 billion in insurance losses, making it one of the largest insured events ever. The World Trade Center disaster cost New Yorkers as much as $105 billion, which includes $34 billion property damage and up to $60 billion in economic costs. The terror attack also took a costly toll in its aftermath, apart from the damage to property and lives. For instance, the abrupt fall in consumer spending and travelling following the attacks exacted a brutal price on business. The stock market lost $1.38 trillion during the first week of trading since September 11. The drop in the Dow Jones industrial average was the biggest weekly slide since the Great Depression of the 1930s. The airline industry in September alone lost $5 billion. Luxury hotels in Mumbai (India), the Taj and Oberoi Trident, were targeted by terrorists on November 26, 2008, which claimed 200 lives besides damaged property. General insurers suffered a loss of more than Rs500 crores ($97 million) due to the Mumbai terror attacks, according to the Insurance Regulatory and Development Authority (IRDA). "This is the biggest estimated loss to the Terror Pool since its inception", IRDA said in its annual report for the year 2008-09. Other attacks in cities like the Bali Indonesia, London, Milan, Mumbai, Delhi and many others, though smaller in size, have taken a huge toll of the respective economies. The emergence of ship hijacking around the waters of Somalia in the Gulf are threatening to disrupt the global shipment of oil from the Persian Gulf and are in part responsible for the hike in both oil and oil transportation rates globally

The astonishing speed with which major corporations become insolvent in the aftermath of the terrorist attacks bears out the importance of accounting for the unpredictable and preparing for uncertainties. Companies need to create bigger cash reserves to weather any external shocks.

Treatment for External Viruses

External viruses are harder to eliminate because they are generated from outside the organisation. Sometimes even having a strong management team will not help to eradicate the external viruses totally. Thomas J. Watson Jr., the head of IBM, in his book *A Business and Its Belief,* told an interviewer that he was afraid IBM would become a big and inflexible organisation that would not be able to keep up with the changes in the computer industry. He said this 30 years before the arrival of Bill Gates and Steve Jobs. Watson was right. IBM (in the pre-Gerstner days) almost went bust in the 1990s. Although mighty IBM had a highly motivated and skilled management team coupled with a very strong brand reputation, it could not withstand the onslaught of personal computers. Then IBM had a corporate culture of arrogance and, to its own peril, ignored the threats of personal computers.

2010 ' Corporate Turnaround Centre

For instance, Gates approached IBM for some collaboration several times during the early days of Microsoft. IBM rejected them all and perhaps could have owned Microsoft today if some of Gates' proposals had been accepted, as Gates was then vulnerable to an acquisition bid by IBM. When IBM woke up to the serious threat of the PC, Gates was financially much stronger and unwilling to part with Windows. IBM was fortunate in its timely recruitment of Lou Gerstner as chairman and CEO to rescue IBM.

Many others were not so lucky. The data bore out the demise of other major companies. Of the Fortune 500 companies of 1970, only a third exists today Many went by the wayside because of their inability to cope with change caused by the attacks of external viruses. The treatment to administer in order to eradicate external viruses is to foster a strong and healthy corporate culture, which is the immune system of the company. The immune system produces antibodies to eradicate the viruses.

In accordance with medical science, developing a strong immune system is the best way to fight viruses, even better than taking drugs. Using the medical analogy, Traditional Chinese Medicine (TCM) appears to be a good way to exterminate external viruses. This is because TCM emphasizes the strengthening of the immune system for preventive, holistic, individualized treatment targeting at the root cause. On the other hand, Western medicine is more effective for treating the symptoms than eliminating viruses. More details of this are discussed in Module #6.

EXERCISE 1.3
ASSESSMENT OF EXTERNAL VIRUSES

STAGE ONE:

Use the table and 6-point scale below to rate the current impact of the following external viruses on your company's performance and fiscal health.

EXTERNAL VIRUSES	IMPACT					
	None	Low	~	Moderate	~	High
	0	1	2	3	4	5
Government intervention/regulations						
Economic recession						
Political turmoil						
Low-cost competitors						
Appreciating/depreciating currencies						
Changes in consumer behaviour						
Environmental/health issues						
Technological changes						
Natural disasters						
Shortage of workers/raw materials						
Labour unrest						
Terrorist attacks						

2010 ' Corporate Turnaround Centre

STAGE TWO:

Now identify the priority issues for action under each internal virus heading.

Government intervention/regulations

Economic recession

Political turmoil

Low-cost competitors

Appreciating/depreciating currencies

Changes in consumer behaviour

Environmental/health issues

Technological changes

Natural disasters

Shortage of workers/raw materials

Labour unrest

Terrorist attacks

2010 ' Corporate Turnaround Centre

STAGE THREE:

Assess the treatment that you have administered so far to tackle these internal viruses:

What steps have you already taken to improve the performance and fiscal health of your company?

What has been the impact/effectiveness of these actions?

What next steps do you expect to take; and when?

2010' Corporate Turnaround Centre

COMPETITION

Era of Competition

The management mantra in the 1970s and 1980s was product quality and activities involving Quality Control (QC) circles, Total Quality Management (TQM) and ISO 9000 with all of them being the order of the day. Back then, consumers were willing to spend enormous sums for quality products.

However, most of the competitors' quality has improved and today, having a good quality product is a given and mandatory requirement for the company to effectively participate and survive in the marketplace. Subsequently in the 1980s and 1990s, the management slogan embraced technology as the cure-all, as having quality products and services no longer ensured survival in the dog-eat-dog business environment. Companies then tried to distinguish themselves from their competitors through the use of technology, by offering better and more features, use of the Internet and communication systems, etc. Huge amounts of funds as well as human resources were channelled into technology and research and development (R&D) in an effort to build a better mousetrap with better state-of-the-art features. Today, a better mousetrap may not necessarily enable you to catch more mice than your competitors, as they too know how to build better mousetraps. For example, the video player has been transformed into a sophisticated multiple-function gadget incorporating several advanced technological innovations, such as video CD and DVD. At times, these sophisticated features become so complicated that most users are confused and unable to operate them easily without flipping through a thick instruction manual. For instance, many users still fumble with trying to record a television programme scheduled to be shown a couple of hours later.

2010' Corporate Turnaround Centre

"The world does not beat down the door of the better mousetrap developer."

The technology philosophy then gradually shifted to emphasise competition, more competition and nothing but competition in the new millennium. The business environment is evolving rapidly each day with advances in communication, transportation, logistics and computer technology. Competition intensifies with the emergence of a better range of products, quality and technology as well as even more attractive pricing. Every product is becoming like a commodity and pricing becomes a key determinant in a shrinking market. Similar to heart ailment or cardiac disease, which is a major killer in developed countries, competition is the major cause of failure for many companies. It is also a silent and sudden killer, like a heart attack, as oftentimes a competitor will creep up on you without your initially realizing it. It is also a highly preventable disease: for the individual through a healthy lifestyle; and for the company, to be always alert and have strategies to combat competition. When you are faced with increasing competition, you may still survive, prosper and succeed, but it cannot be business as usual.

Competitors can catch up on core competencies. Benchmarking and re-engineering may put them on the cutting edge. But only dedicated individuals can continually produce new, creative and exciting ideas that allow a company to reinvent itself, manage its self-renewal process, and foster a true learning organisation. Yet, many companies still fail to use the right management and leadership strategies to motivate and retain their staff.

Where is the Global Economy Going?

Compounding the problem of intense competition is the uncertainty of the global economy. It is uncertain where the global economy is going. During this downturn, countries that have huge domestic markets will stand to suffer relatively less. These include the BRIC[3], Indonesia, Latin America, South Africa etc. Middle Eastern countries are expected to do better as oil prices are still increasing. The recovery in American and European economies is still nascent and they may yet slip back into recession. With data from U.S. consumer spending still weak, most people do not expect a speedy recovery. The confidence of the world in the U.S. dollar as a reserve currency is shaken, given the high levels of debt the U.S. government has built up as a result of the fiscal stimulus that the Obama government has initiated. The ability of China as a global powerhouse which might lead the world to economic recovery is limited. In the build up to the Beijing Olympics, the Chinese government spent large amounts to build infrastructure and continues to build the same at a rapid pace, however, this may not suffice to pull the world out of recession.

The ASEAN countries will need to drastically reorient their economies from being U.S. centric to China centric. The recent agreement for a Free Trade Area between China and ASEAN, and between ASEAN and India will create large trading blocs which cover more than a third of the world population. ASEAN, India and China as a bloc, powered by China can be the next big economic bloc. Hong Kong, Taiwan and South Korea also need to provide aggressive stimulation to their domestic economies instead of merely relying on their exports to the U.S., as the latter is no longer as robust. Furthermore, many countries in South-east Asia need to undergo major structural changes in their economies. The changes facing them no longer are cyclical in nature but long-term threats from other efficient low-cost emerging countries such as China and India. Many of these reforms will be painful treatments and bitter

---

[3] Brazil, Russia, India and China

2010 ' Corporate Turnaround Centre

medicines, difficult to implement and highly unpopular among the populace. Unfortunately, they are a necessary panacea to nurse these economies back to health.

Until September 2008, Asian markets had believed they would not be affected by the situation of Western finance. This is because the emerging economies of today have their own strong domestic markets besides high currency reserves, as well as their good, balanced macroeconomic policies. The economic crisis on Wall Street has further strengthened this fact that Asians have indeed decreased their dependency on the economic conditions of the West. Though it is a fact that all Asian economies, especially in their financial sectors, have been hit by this financial crisis of the West, but the impact has been less severe than what is visible in the U.S. or Europe.

Dubai is still reeling from its worst ever financial crisis. On November 26, 2009, Dubai World – the investment vehicle for the Emirate – asked to delay for six months payment on $26 billion of debt. The extent of the debt rattled many markets causing many indices to drop; including oil prices. U.S. stocks fell sharply but rebounded from their lows as investors concluded that the damage might be contained. Oil prices plunged as much as 7 percent before recovering.

In the first weeks of 2010, renewed anxiety about the excessive levels of debt in some EU countries and, more generally, about the health of the Euro, has spread from Ireland and Greece to Portugal, Spain and Italy. The Greek economy faces its most severe crisis after 1993, with the highest budget deficit (although close to those of Ireland and the UK) as well as the second highest debt to GDP ratio in the EU. The 2009 budget deficit stood at 12.7% of its GDP. This and rising debt levels (113% of GDP in 2009) led to rising borrowing costs, resulting in a severe economic crisis.

Japan, and other Asian "tiger economies" like South Korea, Taiwan, Hong Kong, Vietnam and Malaysia had a large percentage of their economy dependent on exports to the west; these have been badly hit.

Today China faces its largest economic crisis since the Great Depression. Unemployment in rural areas is on the rise. The main reason for this is being cited as too much reliance on exports. Hence, today as an alternative and to boost the economy, the focus is being changed to expanding the domestic market. Various policy measures are being taken to boost economic growth for the country. The post-depression stimulus and the heavy investment made in infrastructure for the Beijing Olympics and now also in the interiors help keep the Chinese economy growing.

The Chinese economy is too reliant on the US economy for its own good. The Chinese Government owns some 2 trillion USD of U.S. debts and any depreciation of the USD is going to deplete the reserves of the Chinese coffers. Also, the Chinese economy still heavily depends on exports to the U.S. Going forward this is not healthy as the U.S. recession is not expected to recover soon. On the positive note, the China has huge foreign reserves which they can use as a fiscal stimulus to prime the pump of the economy. Also, the saving grace is, if the Chinese consumers can start spending, it will jump-start the Chinese economy to become less reliant on the U.S.

Home, Internet and multi-layer marketing businesses are expected to blossom. The crisis has accelerated this process - people are retrenched and stay at home, companies cut back on office rental and operate from homes instead, people stay home to save money. When people stay at home, they will use online entertainment, purchases, communications, and start home businesses. This is why the Internet companies such as Google, eBay and Amazon as well as network marketing businesses are still doing well although many traditional businesses have taken a setback.

2010 ' Corporate Turnaround Centre

Other businesses that typically perform well during a recession include risk management, liquidation, litigation, pawn shops, counter-trade, second-hand goods, etc.

Going Back to the Basics

Whatever the outcome of the global economy, one thing is certain: the business world of today has been described as being in "perpetual white water". It is a good metaphor. Deregulation, globalisation and technological advances are generally remarkable upheavals in both organisations and products – upheavals that none of us could have envisaged even a few years ago. Waves of consolidation are routinely followed by waves of divestitures and restructuring.

It is a small wonder that in many industries, excess capacity is becoming the norm rather than the exception. This is why many companies are falling sick due to intense competition, over-supply and excessive investment everywhere. The best bet for these troubled economies is to restructure their ailing companies to face the new harsh realities. They need to go back to the basics of rebuilding their fiscal health and quickly restructuring themselves in order to handle these challenges head-on. For instance, many unprofitable businesses in Japan and China need to close down in order to not further weaken the banking systems.

For centuries, men have tried in vain to seek the fountain of youth or the magical elixir of long life. The first emperor of China, Qin Shi Huang (259–209 BC), who was brutal and wicked, ordered 500 men and women to find the fountain of youth for him. They were not allowed to return to their families until they found it. These men and women, as expected, did not return and Qin Shi Huang died. Similarly, there is no such fountain of youth for sick economies and companies. However, by availing themselves of the three-phased prescription listed below, they can boost their anti-aging DHEA[4] level, which will short-circuit their attainment of corporate longevity.

In addition, if a company is stricken with illness as depicted in the earlier part of this chapter, it will also need to seek the three-phased medical treatment immediately in order to ensure a speedy recovery. Any delay might bring forth dire consequences. Therefore, the corporate rescue treatment can be classified into three phases:

- Phase I: **Surgery**, with the primary focus on restructuring the organisation and improving the cash flow
- Phase II: **Resuscitation**, with a concentration on revitalizing the business's top line and profit
- Phase III: **Therapy**, with the aim of rehabilitating a strong and healthy corporate immune system for sustained long-term growth

These three phases are described in detail in subsequent chapters using actual turnaround experiences in three classic examples – local as well as foreign companies based in Singapore. These are supplemented by other examples from world-class companies. For complete corporate recovery, one should complete the full course of antibiotics prescribed in treatments of Phase I, II and III. The next small steps involve more analysis, and then learning to balance productivity and innovation.

---

[4] *DeHydroEpiAndrosterone* or the fountain of youth hormones

EXERCISE 1.4

21 Commandments SWOT ANALYSIS

SWOT stands for **s**trengths, **w**eaknesses, **o**pportunities, and **t**hreats. Strengths and weaknesses are typically internal factors while opportunities and threats are external.

STAGE ONE:

Based on the 21 Commandments in the table below, identify whether each statement is a strength, a weakness, an opportunity for growth, or a threat to the success of your company's operations and future success.

21 COMMANDMENTS	Internal Factors		External Factors	
	Strength	Weakness	Opportunity	Threat
Recognition of the problem				
Accept responsibility for the problem				
Be willing to work to bring change/success				
Prepare to take early intervention				
Regular check/updates are needed				
To know the cause is to only know part of the solution				
Consider that past practices may be the root of the company's problems				
Know your stakeholders – competitors, customers and market				
Know the company well in order to understand the problem				

(Continued over the page...)

(Continued from previous page...)

21 COMMANDMENTS	Internal Factors		External Factors	
	Strength	Weakness	Opportunity	Threat
Communicate and closely monitor expectations				
Simplify and clearly communicate strategies and assessments for change				
Learn quickly for yourself and from the experiences of others				
Stay up to date on the business activities and strategies of your competitors				
Be aware of problems in your business so that your competitors cannot take advantage of your errors				
Know your markets to match quality, pricing and service				
Do not allow competitors to gain a position in your market, with your customers or your suppliers				
Provide and reward accurate and timely oral and written communications regarding the company's work and employees				
Resolve employee, partner and shareholder issues and concerns quickly in order to protect the corporate environment				
Stop rumours quickly regarding people, the company, the market and the economy				
Require competency and commitment from all levels of the company				
Board members are competent, committed and focused on the corporate vision and mission				

2010 ' Corporate Turnaround Centre

STAGE TWO:

Based on the results of your SWOT analysis of the "21 Commandments", are most of the issues with your company:

Internal factors (strengths, weaknesses) or external factors (opportunities, threats)?

Related to relationships?

Related to fiscal accountability?

Other issues? Identify the other issues.

2010 ' Corporate Turnaround Centre

EXERCISE 1.5

SUMMARY OF MODULE #1

Taking Module #1 as a whole and looking back over the sections on:

- Physical and Fiscal Health – The Medical Analogy
- Why Do Companies Fail
- Corporate Viruses
- Competition
- The 21 Commandments

And, of course, the outcomes of your exercises, please answer for yourself the following questions:

What are your company's <u>four</u> areas of greatest strength?

1.

2.

3.

4.

What are your company's <u>four</u> areas of greatest concern?

1.

2.

3.

4.

Considering the actions you may already have taken to improve the performance and fiscal health of your company, summarise in the table below your key future actions for improvement:

Short Term	Medium Term	Long Term

Defining a Culture of Productivity and Innovation

We have nearly completed our diagnosis. However, to identify an illness, the doctor also needs to have a picture of "wellness". What would the patient look like, if he were healthy instead of ailing?

This section describes a healthy, well-balanced corporation: one pursuing both productivity and innovation.

As a runner develops stress injuries if one leg is longer than the other...or if she always runs the same way on an inclined track, so one foot reaches the ground sooner than the other...so too a corporation will damage itself if it does not balance both innovation and productivity.

This chapter will describe in greater detail:
- Why a focus on productivity will ultimately fail
- Why innovation alone might not produce profits
- How to create a corporate culture that innovates productively and also pursues productivity in innovative ways.

2010 ' Corporate Turnaround Centre

The Productivity of Innovation

Industry needs many drivers, not just one alone
Everything must fall into place, the tasks must be done
Making products, and making them fast
Is not everything to making companies last

Innovation can be priceless but it is not everything
Innovation can transform business and make them sing
But only if it has the backing from all concerned
Will it provide a guide for how money is to be earned

Business needs to be productive in innovative ways
This will make a company do well, and start to pay
One without the other will lead to decline
One without the other will not toe the line

The Corporate transformation index shows the way
To get the most from innovation and productivity today
There are many questions that will reveal
If a company's innovation culture is the real deal

Innovation often comes from the past
These ideas are good and built to last
Creativity, hard work, flair, and desire
Make old products new that set the world on fire

The world is competitive in all of its markets
It needs to make the most from all its facets
This way it can innovate and make packets
And be productive, and set good price brackets

Sometimes in business, many questions are raised
And it all looks confusing, and can leave people dazed
Concentration is needed and a guiding hand
Can keep businesses out of the bad land

Mistakes from the past can be our guide
Many failed projects, we can stay wide
Through learning the mistakes we can save our hide
If we hit stormy seas, we can turn the tide

Innovation and productivity hold all the answers
To create companies, those are healthy money makers

2010 ' Corporate Turnaround Centre

Corporate transformation has given us the key
To have the best and healthy companies

Invest in the cultures of innovation and productivity
And business booms and companies see profitability
This is the way forward, to be competitive
Staying ahead of the game, while staying innovative

2010 ' Corporate Turnaround Centre

ENHANCING PRODUCTIVITY INNOVATIVELY AND INNOVATION PRODUCTIVELY

Introduction

The Singapore government has identified productivity and innovation as the twin drivers to transform Singapore's economy in the years ahead. This is the right direction to take: both are needed. In today's very competitive world, productivity tools alone are not enough, as most of these tools have been known and used by our competitors for many years. Innovation alone is also not adequate. There are many innovative initiatives out there in the marketplace and mostly not making money. Beyond innovating, important steps include implementing and commercializing those innovations productively and profitably. Thus, in short, we need to improve efficiency effectively or to improve productivity innovatively (cheaper and faster) and innovation productively (better and breaking bottlenecks).

The former helps to produce products/services cheaper and faster and the latter introduces better products/services and break bottlenecks that hinder progress.

Singapore companies

This concept of improving productivity innovatively and innovation productively will be very relevant for our companies. Most small medium sized enterprises (SMEs) in Singapore play a middle-man role: traders, distributors, agencies, sub-contractors, sub-manufacturers and more. This business model is becoming obsolete with the onset of internet , modern –day infocomm and

2010 ' Corporate Turnaround Centre

globalisation. The role of the middle-man is being marginalised as it is very easy for the manufacturers to approach the customers directly. And with the pressures on margins, both buyers and sellers want to deal directly and avoid paying the middle-man unless there is value-added contribution from the middle-man. Thus, becoming more productive in a losing business model does not help. At best it helps prolong the business in the short term. It is not practical for our SMEs to become manufacturers or totally change their business models immediately. Our SMEs need to use innovation to re-position, resuscitate or reinforce the business models so that it will be a profitable one and able to handle the new realities in the marketplace.

Productivity Alone

Often companies will focus on productivity. Productivity deals with the basic economics of production: how many widgets can we manufacture at what cost, and how quickly? Improved productivity can lead to increased profitability, but only if the market for these widgets remains strong.

There is little point in becoming more productive in a obsolete product or an agency that is going to be taken away. You may have developed a productive method of making telex machines per hour – but what is the global demand for telex machines when personal computers can do the job and offer more functions? If the manufacturers are planning to market on their own or to take over the agency, more productivity will not save the day. An example is our Cycle and Carriage which lost the Merc agency not because they are not good enough but the manufacturer has other reasons.

2010 ' Corporate Turnaround Centre

Innovation Alone

Almost every organization can tap into a deep well of innovation. From the classic suggestion box to modern intra-net databases, a company can easily ask employees to recommend improvements. Beyond these incremental changes, an R&D department has the mandate to develop new products or methodologies. These innovative initiatives are not enough. innovation is defined as a good idea that gets implemented productively and profitably.

The vexing question is : "Can we make a profit with this innovation"?

Where has innovation failed when it stood alone?
- GM (General Motors), like most automakers, does introduce innovative products and features. They are roundly criticized for the time it takes from conception to market. Smaller car makers have been able to deliver much more quickly – and thereby take market share away from GM.
- Although X-rays were generated from Crookes tubes as early as 1875, and detected in 1895, it was not until the 20th century that medical or commercial applications were developed.
- More recently, the "dot.com" bust showed that creative individuals and innovative companies may attract capital investment but fail to deliver a profit.
- Trek Technology and IBM began selling the first USB flash drives commercially in 2000. The Singaporean Trek Technology sold a model under the brand name "ThumbDrive" which became a household name. Unfortunately, most companies that manufacture USB flash drives do so without regard for Trek's patent. The question is how Trek Technology can make its innovation more productive by protecting it from other copycat manufacturers. Incidentally, this is also a major problem for many innovative products as to how the innovators can protect their products when some countries do not respect intellectual property rights.

2010' Corporate Turnaround Centre

Enhancing Productivity Innovatively

Productivity emphasis alone is not enough to give Singapore the competitive advantage over the Chinese, Indians and Eastern Europeans with lower labour costs and they too have learned the productivity skills and tools. In the context of Singapore, productivity needs to be innovatively implemented.

Sometimes success flows to those who use someone else's productive and innovative invention in creative ways. This is something that Singapore companies may want to follow in adapting and leveraging its existing business model innovatively. Several examples of such companies are:

- The "mp3" concept was invented by Singapore's Creative Technology. That company is not currently doing well financially as compared to Apple. Apple Computers, however, continues to embed "mp3" in its iPod and other products. Steve Jobs succeeds because Apple products serve the lifestyle aspirations of its customers.

- Talent shows have long been a staple of television; that innovation was made in the past. The "Idol" group – such as American Idol – has added the innovation of audience voting in near-real time. This uses supporting technologies such as pay-per-call telephone numbers and texting to increase the viewers' identification with "their" contestants.

- Radio and television have presented news shows since their earliest days. Ted Turner invented the 24-hour news channel. And CNN is a great success though it is still news but brought to you 24 hours. This is now a crowded but profitable niche in the multi-channel world of television: 24 hour sports programming; 24 hour drama; comedy and so on.

- Google and eBay are two examples of companies which combine innovation and productivity to produce solid profits. Google, in particular,

2010 ' Corporate Turnaround Centre

continues to make innovative advances in search engines; and it drives productivity by investing in data centres throughout the world. Google did not invent the search engine nor the data centre; but they continually strive to improve them through innovation in new offerings such as Google Adwords, Google Earth, Google Analytics and other Google applications

Enhancing Innovation Productively

There are many R&D projects that are losing money because the products are either not commercially viable, too early for its time or simply not marketed at all.

- The Charles Schwab Corporation exemplifies ongoing and profitable innovation. It is credited   with providing discounted brokerage services by removing investment advice from a retail stock transaction; 24X7 automated telephone brokerage services; a PC-based program for retail clients to research and trade shares; and more. Part of the credit goes to "Charles Schwab's Guiding Principles": a framework for making decisions about potential innovations.
- Salesforce.com uses the cloud computing, an innovative tool in a productive manner to capture the customer relationship management market by increasing productivity for customers.
- Samsung began its business by imitating successful products made by its competitors. More recently it has emphasized the importance of innovation. The process includes encouraging creativity by individuals and also disseminating the innovation across the company, but in disciplined and structured ways. And now Samsung has overtaken Sony in the electronic consumer market share.

Both Productivity and Innovation

Look back at these successes. Innovations may have been technological, such as the mp3 player; or oriented to combining services and technologies in new ways as in the talent show.

However, these innovations required significant productivity improvements. Imagine a 1950's talent show that would ask for audience voting. A large call centre would be dedicated to taking phone calls and tabulating the results on paper. Or the show would take at least a week to announce the results of a mail-in ballot.

Could CNN exist in a world with 12 broadcast channels? Would they ever have been given an initial broadcast license? The technological innovation of "more channels" led to experimentation and opportunity. However, CNN would not have survived without its 24 hour feature.

Success and profitability require both innovation and productivity. What new product or service can we develop? How can we deliver it? Will it be easy to find a market? Can we scale up to meet rising demand?

Only by pursuing the twin goals of productivity and innovation can a company gain and retain a competitive edge. New and innovative methods for improving productivity are required, since other organizations also seek ways to cut costs and produce more with less. Applying systematic productivity tools to the task of creating innovations will be required, since other competitors are busy inventing new products which may render yours obsolete.

In conclusion, what Singapore needs most is not increasing productivity or innovation alone but improving productivity innovatively and innovation productively shall be the key thrust for our economy.

Measuring Productivity and Innovation

Tom DeMarco said "You can't control what you can't measure" in "*Controlling Software Projects: Management, Measurement and Estimation.*"

Business management gurus promote many productivity measures. Here are a few:

- Productivity = number of goods produced during a work shift (or week, or year)
- Productivity = dollar value of goods produced during a work shift (or week, or year)
- Productivity = dollar value of goods produced divided by the costs of labour and materials, etc.
- Productivity = profits realized per work shift (or week, etc.) in a fiscal reporting period
- Productivity = revenues realized, divided by costs, in a fiscal reporting period

Can we apply similar measurements for innovation? Consider these candidates for an Innovation Index (II):

- II = number of innovations suggested during a week, quarter or year
- II = number of innovations adopted during a week, quarter or year
- II = number of innovations, per employee, adopted during a week, quarter or year

2010 ' Corporate Turnaround Centre

- II = number of innovations, <u>divided by corporate profits</u>, adopted during a week, quarter or year (for example, 3 innovations per million dollars of profit)
- II = dollars invested in R&D, <u>divided by corporate budget</u>, in a fiscal reporting period
- II = <u>profits attributed to last year's innovations</u>, divided by overall corporate profits

If your company uses a Balanced Scorecard, be sure to include a Productivity index and an Innovation Index.

Finally, use a combined Corporate Transformation Index by multiplying a Productivity Index by the Innovation Culture index. For example, productivity measured as the Output/Input multiply by the Innovation Culture Index percentage which is Total innovation culture scores/Total innovation culture scale (which is measured on a Levitt scale). Over time, the Corporate Transformation Index should rise due to improvements in both productivity and innovation culture indexes.

Transformation Equals Productivity Times Innovation

Productivity deals with the basic economics of production. How many widgets can we manufacture, at what cost, and how quickly? Improved productivity can lead to increased profitability, but only if the market for these widgets remains strong.

Innovation deals with improving products or services, or creating new ones. Almost every organization can tap into a deep well of innovation. From the classic suggestion box to modern intranet databases, a company can easily ask employees to recommend improvements. Beyond these incremental changes, an R&D department has the mandate to develop new products or methodologies.

However, an Innovation Culture goes far beyond haphazard creativity. Just as manufacturers have adopted a variety of productivity disciplines, such as Six Sigma or 5S, so must every organization build a set of processes to pursue innovation in an orderly and repeatable fashion. Like the productivity disciplines, innovation should be founded with budgets, processes and expectations.

As noted above, Google combines productivity and innovation to produce profits. By continual innovation in search engines and other software, and by ongoing productivity investments to improve its data centers throughout the world, Google maintains and increases its advantages over its competitors.

To achieve success and profitability, both productivity and innovation are required. A company's continuing quest is to develop new products or services; to deliver them in newer, faster and more cost-effective ways; to find new markets and build market share; and to meet the rising demand.

Remember that business management gurus promote many productivity measures, such as:

- Productivity = dollar value of goods produced divided by the costs of labour and materials, etc.

  We can apply similar measurements for innovation, such as:

- Innovation Index = dollars invested in R&D, divided by corporate budget, in a fiscal reporting period

The **Innovation Culture in Ninety Questions** ™ provides the tools to measure "Innovation Culture". This document also includes several sample questions, split among the three phases of corporate recovery in sections:

- "Innovation Culture Measurements for Phase 2 Part 2" (after exercise 5.1)
- "Innovation Culture Measurements for Phase 3 Part 1" (after exercise 6.1)

2010 ' Corporate Turnaround Centre

- "Innovation Culture Measurements for Phase 3 Part 2" (after exercise 8.1)

This document provides the tools to measure **productivity**. See the following sections:
- "Productivity Measurements for Phase 1" (after exercise 2.2)
- "Productivity Measurements for Phase 2 Part 1" (after exercise 3.1)
- "Productivity Measurements for Phase 3 Part 1" (after exercise 6.1)

Together, these two indices give a numeric value to the organization's culture of productivity and innovation.

END OF MODULE #1

With the diagnosis completed, you should now have a clear idea of your company's strengths and weaknesses and where your priority issues lie. In the next module, we look at the first phase of the corporate turnaround process, which is Surgery.

~

Additional Online Resources

The following books authored by Dr. Mike Teng are relevant to module #1, covering Diagnosis. Details are available by clicking on the website below for each book.

Corporate Turnaround: Nursing a sick company back to health

www.miketeng.com

Using medical analogies, *Corporate Turnaround: Nursing a Sick Company Back to Health* prescribes effective and easy-to-administer turnaround techniques in the right doses.

Business Diagnosis

www.restructuringcosts.com

This book provides a guide on how to determine the corporate health. It also provides a list of cost-cutting measures to help company manage its cash flow

Inspirational Notebook

www.inspirationalnotebook.com

A book to inspire and encourage companies for corporate transformation and turnaround with poems, YouTube videos and books outlines. A good companion to have for one's note-taking as well.

Also visit Dr. Mike Teng's www.youtube.com/1103teng **to watch the YouTube videos of some of the books.**

Transformation Presentation 1

http://tinyurl.com/Transformationpresentation1

Most companies today need to go through corporate turnaround and transformation. Yet, many companies do not know how because they have not met such a protracted crisis like this one before. And many business schools do not teach the subject of corporate turnaround and transformation because many academic staff members do not have this experience. This protracted recession can mean significant challenges and problems to companies. Stay away from such a desperate situation and save your company from the trouble of having to deal with a depression RIGHT NOW! The solution is to learn from the expert on how to manage the challenges. Avoid making the same mistakes that other people have made on restructuring. This talk not only shares how to restructure but also restructure into a competitive, innovative and flexible organization. This is part 1 of 3.

Transformation Presentation 2

http://tinyurl.com/Transformationpresentation2

This is part 2 of 3 in the series on corporate turnaround and transformation.

Transformation Presentation 3

http://tinyurl.com/Transformationpresentation3

This concludes the 3-part series on corporate turnaround and transformation.

Best-selling corporate turnaround books

http://tinyurl.com/turnaroundbooks

Corporate turnaround and transformation are essential in this global economic depression. Change management is the first step to be taken towards restoring and ensuring the health of companies that have been affected by this financial crisis. From a series of best-selling books by Dr. Michael Teng, you can learn everything there is to know about corporate turnaround, buying and selling companies, office politics, personal transformation and beating competition in cyberspace.

Early diagnosis

http://tinyurl.com/earlydiagnosis

With this comprehensive toolkit you can determine the health of your organization as of a particular date. Use this handbook to identify possible symptoms of poor health early on. Probe deep into specific weak spots, prescribe solutions to fix the problems, prioritize the focus areas and treat with appropriate remedies.

MODULE #2

PHASE ONE: BREAKING THE BOTTLENECK: SURGERY: FOCUS ON PRODUCTIVITY

"Change Management"

Do you have a business that isn't doing what it should?
Do you have a business that isn't doing any good?
Companies need to check their health,
So they can start to generate wealth,

Surgery, resuscitation and therapy
Are proven business methods, just wait and see
Go with our guidance and go with our words
And get your business out there, get your name heard

So don't despair my friend, as now you know why
We're here to save it all, and make your business fly
All you need is a new set of wings
With a little change management you can do amazing things

There's no need to be scared – this is no business muscle
We're just here to add common sense to the everyday hustle
Let me be clear, it isn't plain sailing
But it will be worth it if it's your business we're saving

So jump aboard this train, the fare isn't too steep
Jump aboard this train, before you start to weep
Business turnaround is the name of the game
Change management is our name.

2010 ' Corporate Turnaround Centre

WHAT IS THE SURGICAL PHASE?

Surgery or corporate restructuring is not a slash-and-burn exercise. Rather it calls for a surgeon's skills that are characterized by the **four Cs**:

- **C**ommunication
- **C**oncentration
- **C**ost Control
- **C**ash Flow

COMMUNICATION

When a company gets into difficulties, it is a matter of time before those difficulties become common knowledge. To avoid misunderstanding and stalling the turnaround plan, it is important that the turnaround CEO makes Cost Control - his internal and external communication plans – known clearly to the parties involved. The best form of communication is to practise what you preach: walk the talk.

Just as a medical doctor should not delegate to the nurse the task of informing a patient about the nature of his ailment and the required treatment, the turnaround CEO should *personally* inform the staff of the turnaround plans. Key steps in the communication process encompass the following:

1. Form a turnaround team
2. Enlist support
3. Apply a no-nonsense management style

Form a Turnaround Team

Foremost in the communication process is the formation of the turnaround team. Turnarounds are seldom one-person shows. Most well-orchestrated corporate comeback teams are fielded with the best talents from within or outside the company, including skilled professionals such as insolvency lawyers, auditors and turnaround consultants. The first step for creating a successful change is to get everyone on board. If they believe that what you are doing will lead to a better future, the employees will make an effort to ensure that these changes work. It is the members of the turnaround team that execute the details of operations for restructuring the corporation.

It is also vital that the turnaround CEO communicate to the staff in a clear manner about the company's troubled circumstances and the urgent need for implementation of some tough albeit unpopular measures in order to reverse its fortunes and forestall any further deterioration in the company's ailing health. For example, the restructuring is necessary because of the general economic slowdown, failures of product launches or investments, or loss of big accounts, etc. You should tell it like it is, early and honestly. Some rough time-frames on the restructuring process could also be given if the turnaround CEO is able to offer this. The purpose of the communication process is to get employees to work with you productively during such tough times.

As such, this part of the surgical phase should be speedy, as time is of the essence. Undue delays in communicating the turnaround plan may generate uncertainties and insecurities that subsequently could lead to an exodus of better staff. Unlike some turnaround CEOs, who have a revolving door for executives and managers, the turnaround team should be changed only if it is not working out. Constant changes make it difficult to build rapport and know the team members well. Whenever possible, bring in trusted and reliable people who have been with you before, mature men and women who can work with you as a team. As rapport has already been established and they are

2010 ' Corporate Turnaround Centre

acquainted with your style, things get done faster. In that way, there is a lesser degree of misunderstanding and mistrust. Time is of the essence. You need to get things done quickly and full support must be rendered to you by the turnaround team.

The CEO must look for people who can complement their professional and personal attributes, have lots of creative ideas and are able to implement them – people who have been through change before and can assist as change agents. Also, people who are able to take criticism and who will speak up when the process goes off the track are assets to the process. Many unpopular and politically incorrect decisions may need to be taken. Popularity is a cheap way to buy respect, but it does not last. The only way to get respect is to be successful and deliver results.

Enlist Support

Often, turnaround CEOs are not given full autonomy, especially if they are new to the organization. They have to earn the trust and support of various parties in order to be able to execute their job well. It is therefore important to enlist the support of stakeholders, such as top management, shareholders, union and staff. This is because during the course of the turnaround, there will be unpopular measures taken that will affect them directly or indirectly. As such, it is mandatory that the turnaround CEO keep them informed of the turnaround plan and regularly update them on the progress made. Failure to do so may breed disquiet or sabotage, thereby jeopardizing the turnaround process.

Unity at this juncture is paramount, as the turnaround CEO's attention and energy should not be diverted to fight unproductive battles waged by dissenting stakeholders. You need to have some amount of autonomy to perform the corporate surgery effectively. However, the right to autonomy quite often has got to be earned and gradually entrusted to you by the

2010 ' Corporate Turnaround Centre

shareholders or board of directors when you communicate with them frequently. Give them the assurance that you know what you are doing.

Therefore, before taking up a turnaround assignment, it is imperative to determine whether the chairman is the cause of the company's problem. If this is so, then the turnaround manager should be bold enough to ask the chairman for full executive power. Otherwise, it is advisable not to take up the turnaround assignment, as it will be doomed to fail. Many turnaround efforts may require the firing of staff related to the chairman, such as his close associates and relatives.

Apply a No-nonsense Management Style

During Phase I, ailing organizations are subjected to unpopular and often painful measures, such as changing of Managers (blood transfusion), closing down of operation (blood-letting) or changing of business models (change of DNA), which will not win anyone over. Things will not be the same as before. Changes will be necessary and people in general are resistant to change. Therefore, participative and consensus management is not likely to work during Phase I. The turnaround CEO must be prepared to operate as a benevolent dictator – one who is tough yet reasonable and compassionate. The turnaround team mentioned earlier is there to support this CEO. The authority and responsibility must rest with the CEO. This individual must assume the overall leadership role in this phase and make timely decisions regarding personnel, strategy, investment, and policy matters.

When the problems start at a company, they are often traceable to a management more concerned with its own perks than with the products the company makes or the services it offers. When you make changes, start by doing away with corporate perks such as providing chauffeurs, company cars and first-class air tickets. The directive to reduce cost should commence at the corporate headquarters level, the with primary aim to shrink expensive

2010 ' Corporate Turnaround Centre

unproductive management. A turnaround manager also needs to abide by the ethical code of practice. For instance, a turnaround manager needs to walk the talk. If you throw out the perks and corporate benefits of the managers, you also need to lead by example. For instance, you will lose credibility if you continue to fly business class when you have decided that the managers must downgrade to economy class.

Management is the backbone around which the rest of the staff is shaped. Quite often, internal viruses are allowed to fester because of weak management. If a company is in trouble, for the most part, a company cannot cure itself solely from the inside using the existing management. If management is the cause of the trouble, it usually has too much self-interest to make changes. The ailing company needs to have a change agent or blood transfusion, perhaps a turnaround CEO or new senior manager, preferably someone who is not bogged down by past baggage and who is driven to do what is right for the business no matter what it takes, even at the risk of losing one's own job.

In the surgical phase, you are not in a position to be well-liked. The turnaround manager is here to succeed. He has to succeed for the sake of stakeholders, not just the board of directors and other major investors. The interests of minority investors such as working men and women and retired folks, need to be protected. Morally, the turnaround manager also has to succeed for the sake of the company employees and their families who depend on them. They have entrusted to him the task of leading them out of the rut. If you are going to do a corporate turnaround, you better understand that many poor people depend on you to succeed and that your goal is to make money for them. Indeed, this is an awesome and heavy responsibility.

CONCENTRATION

During the surgical phase, there is time and resource constraint. Therefore, the turnaround CEO needs to concentrate all the resources on doing a few major things right. An ailing company needs to concentrate only on its core competence and try to rid itself of businesses that do not help the bottom-line. This will enable the ailing organization to attain a clear and dedicated focus on what it does best. Also, the effectiveness of management can be improved by scaling the business down to a size that is within its capabilities to manage. Cash flow can also be improved significantly.

Concentration entails:
- Focusing on core competence
- Eliminating marginally profitable projects
- Adopting a zero-based budgeting approach
- Challenging past business assumptions

Many studies in the West have found that focus or concentration is the way to go. Michael Treacy and Fred Wiersema, in their book *"The Discipline of Market Leaders"*, presented a deceptively simple thesis: those successful companies – the market leaders – excel at delivering one type of value to their chosen customers. The key is focus. Market leaders choose a single "value discipline" – best total cost, best product or best total solution – and literally build their organisation around it.

Intel, for example, leverages its core competencies in the processor and semiconductor business based upon market growth for faster and faster processors. Intel's competitive strategy is reflected in their start-up or planning of entries into a number of non-core businesses in order to help ensure continued growth in faster and faster processors. They have quite correctly perceived that demand has begun to wane with the relative stabilization of

2010 ' Corporate Turnaround Centre

clock-cycle-eating software applications. The challenge has become to scrape processor cycle latency back down to zero, thereby increasing demand for more processing power.

Focusing on Core Competence

In an increasingly competitive business environment, the sick company must return to the basics. It needs to concentrate and focus on its core competence, instead of being distracted by the urge to venture into new areas in order to survive. This is usually the only option left for the sick company, as it lacks the financial resources to venture into non-core areas. In order to free up resources for its core business, the ailing company has to divest any unprofitable or non-related businesses. With increased competition and the globalization of business, the future belongs to the company that can narrow its focus in order to dominate its industry. Focus on what you know best!

Eliminating Marginally Profitable Projects

Another avenue to improve the dire cash position of an ailing company is to stop the erosion of resources through unprofitable sidelines, or marginally profitable ones that can tip into non-profitability. Sometimes, the troubled company's sales figures can give a misleading picture of its bottom-line. Therefore, it is essential to review margins of all projects taken on by the company in their proper context. The key is to focus on core competence (described in the earlier section): to reorganize the company into a smaller but more profitable outfit. In addition, the prices of some of the company's products may need to be raised to stem the magnitude of loss. If done correctly, a price increase may have no adverse impact on sales volume. However, this should not be an indiscriminate price increase, but rather the increase must be well-thought-out, well-planned and well-executed. In approaching the price increase, it is important to be market-driven, reflecting the company's perceived position in the marketplace by the customer. Customers must also be given sufficient notice of impending price changes that are backed up with strong documented reasons for any price increase, such as the increase in raw materials and labour costs. Price changes should always be based on price/volume consideration, not emotional constraints.

Adopting a Zero-Based Budgeting Approach

In a turnaround situation, the company does not have the luxury of being able to procure and allocate resources freely as in the previous normal business environment. The turnaround CEO must communicate this clearly to the turnaround management team for eventual dissemination to the other staff of the company. This concept runs against the application of conventional budgeting techniques, such as incremental budgeting, where the respective department budgets its resources by adding an incremental amount to the previous year's budgeted figures. Such increases can be based on a certain benchmark or an arbitrary percentage increase in the next financial period. Hence, the zero-based budgeting approach is introduced. In zero-based budgeting, each manager justifies his proposed activities as if they are being performed for the first time. All costs are analyzed and justified from a base of zero. It does not start with what is in existence now, and can be used to see exactly how much money a unit is spending. In addition, it requires an existing program to justify its existence. Thus, zero-based budgeting is the process of reporting an operating plan or budget that starts with no authorized funds. Each department must be required to prepare its budget based on a start-up environment, and justify the existence of each head count. In this way, each department of the company is conditioned to work as efficiently as possible within the set resource constraints. The message given here is the need to concentrate or focus, since human minds, as well as the company's resources, are limited.

2010 ' Corporate Turnaround Centre

Challenge Old Business Assumptions

In a troubled company, it is prudent to challenge all "sacred cows" or old and sacrosanct business assumptions. It is probable that some of these old "sacred cows" were based on erroneous perceptions and assumptions that eventually got the company into trouble. Traditions and past business assumptions underlying the old ways of doing business may be the root cause of the disease suffered by the ailing company. In times of rapid change, strategic failure is often caused by a crisis of perception that we have gone through this before or falsely assuming that this change is temporary and taking for granted that the impact would not be significant and hence, should be ignored. Many of these old and obsolete assumptions happen in large and well-known companies whose traditional cash-cow businesses have become sacred cows and finally end up as sacrificial cows, or worse, cow dung, when market forces overwhelm them. Time and time again, some wrong business assumptions and perceptions by experts have led many companies astray. To ensure its effective and successful implementation, the turnaround CEO must critically re-examine and revisit every business assumption made by the company in the past. Functioning much like diagnostic tests, such as blood tests, this will initiate a sifting process to identify which of these assumptions actually contributed to the distressed company's existing woes and conundrum. By diligently applying this microscopic examination, fallacious business assumptions can be identified, such as over-reliance on a single supplier who may no longer be competitive. Through outsourcing, costs may be reduced, thereby shoring up profit margins.

EXERCISE 2.1

SURGICAL ACTION PLANNING – PART I

Using the "surgical" processes related to communication and concentration presented in this module, begin the process of developing an action plan for the reorganization of your company. Identify actions that must be taken, the individuals and/or departments that need to be involved and determine the financial commitment required for each strategy.

	Key Steps	Actions	Individuals or Departments	Timeline	Costs or Savings
COMMUNICATION	Form a turnaround team				
	Enlist support				
	Apply a no-nonsense management style				
CONCENTRATION	Focusing on core competence				
	Eliminating marginally profitable projects				
	Adopting a zero-based budgeting approach				
	Challenging past business assumptions				

COST CONTROL

Gaining fiscal control is critical for treating a corporation in crisis. Unnecessary cost is always your enemy number one. You must attack it and justify every expense. If your cost to make something is your competitor's price for selling it, you cannot stay in business for long. You must attack cost in every department, size and amount. Critical considerations include:

- Revised operating budget must be valid
- Delicate balancing act
- One of foremost tasks
- Motivate staff before downsizing
- Strengthen staff in other ways
- Explore other temporary or long-term alternatives to firing staff
- Consider outsourcing specific operations
- Develop multi-disciplinary skills across staff positions
- Consider telecommuting
- Eliminate dysfunctional personnel
- Treat downsized staff well
- Win back trust with excellent communication

Challenge every cost

Cost-control is an important antidote or effective remedy to administer, especially in desperate turnaround situations. It is usually short-term or temporary in nature, requiring across-the-board application for all but the most necessary expenses. To successfully implement cost-control, the cuts must be swift, strong and decisive. Sometimes, it has to be done ruthlessly, as the company's present survival and future growth are at stake. As this part of the restructuring involves making many unpopular decisions, the turnaround CEO must carry this out in a sensitive yet prudent manner. Cost-control covers a wide range of measures but these essentially fall into three main categories:

1. Cutting operating budget
2. Downsizing workforce
3. Reducing fixed and variable overheads

Cutting Operating Budget

One of the first measures commonly undertaken by the turnaround CEO is to immediately reduce head count. However, this may be a nostrum[5] measure and may not achieve the desired results. Thus, reducing head count need not necessarily be the turnaround CEO's first option, as there are many "other ways to skin the cat." Seeking cuts in operating budget is one of the foremost tasks of the turnaround CEO who must do his homework to ensure that the revised operating budget is both valid and workable before implementing it. Since the old budget is no longer valid, the turnaround CEO must draw up a revised operating budget. When deciding upon cuts in the operating budget, the turnaround CEO has to perform the delicate balancing act of determining the desired percentage cut that would be effective in boosting the bottom-line but yet not cripple the company's operations. By performing year-to-year comparisons of the financial statements, the turnaround CEO is able to ascertain whether expenses are in line with current sales. He can then identify the expense items and magnitude of cuts required to achieve break-even or even a small profit. Such analyses are useful in pin-pointing problems. The cost-control process is to be treated as a mission towards accomplishing the company's corporate restructuring goals. If this part of the planning process is amiss, it can create havoc and mess up the entire operation, as the wrong top-line forecast will impact the bottom-line adversely.

---

[5] A nostrum is a medicine which is claimed, falsely, to be effective.

Downsize the Workforce

Prior to trimming the workforce, the turnaround CEO should:

- First seek to motivate the staff to give of their best. Staff reduction, although effective initially, usually results in poor morale and low productivity. Furthermore, such "corporate amputation" (act of cutting off) may cause further escalation in the company's weak fiscal health as "corporate anorexia" (absence of appetite) sets in to decimate the remaining staff by further trimming.
- Downsizing the workforce is only one of many tools available to the CEO and managers to improve a company's performance and decrease costs.

Other alternatives to firing staff in order to reduce staff costs could include:

- Implementing pay cuts.
- Using part-timers instead of full-time staff (thereby saving on medical and paid-leave expenses).
- Combining job functions.
- Scheduling a shorter work module.
- Using "forced" leave.
- Cutting perks and benefits (especially travel, entertainment allowances, etc.).

However, these are largely temporary measures that could buy time for the company during the turnaround process.

In a downsizing exercise that is sometimes necessary to save the company, success will sometimes be measured as much in how you do it as in what you do. For example, try not to reduce the number of lowly paid operators before you trim the headquarters staff. These lowly-paid operators will know that you are serious if you slice the real fat first: Get rid of unproductive senior executives, middle managers and some dysfunctional personnel. Deal with unions and operators last. Employees will be more supportive of cutbacks if it means the general health of the company will be demonstrably improved.

2010 ' Corporate Turnaround Centre

Choose wisely the type of dysfunctional personnel to fire rather than adopt a "one-size fits all" approach. Most managers find firing of their staff the most difficult part of their job.

One such example is that of Eastman Chemical Co., a Fortune 500 company with 2008 sales of $6.7 billion. Headquartered in Kingsport, Tennessee, Eastman employs 10,300 people worldwide, including 6,800 in Kingsport. In 2009, 300 jobs were eliminated companywide, including 200 in Kingsport. Jim Rogers, Eastman CEO said that by reducing high-level jobs, the company flattened its management structure, bringing it in line with the overall size of the company: *"The highest percentage reduction of people was at the vice president (level), and the next highest was at the director level."* Eastman Chief Financial Officer Curt Espeland said the company's work force reduction and other cutbacks *"are improving an already solid financial foundation that will sustain us through even an extended period of weak demand."*

There are two types of dysfunctional personnel in both healthy as well as sick companies. Drawing from the medical parallel, they are:
- Benign tumour cases
- Malignant tumour cases

Benign Tumour Cases
This group involves the many incompetent and unmotivated staff who are unable to find alternative employment. The situation is not entirely healthy and is counterproductive as some of them may complain excessively or even deliberately sabotage the operations by slowing down while awaiting their retrenchment.

Malignant Tumour Cases
This is the more harmful group of all the dysfunctional groups of personnel. It usually involves staff with integrity problems or negative attitudes working actively against the interest of the company. Just as in the case of malignant

2010' Corporate Turnaround Centre

carcinoma (cancer) cells, such people are working against the company all the time. Attempts must be made to eliminate this group as soon as possible.

Recommended Amicable Approach

Despite having to assume the executioner's role, the turnaround CEO should strive to alleviate and minimize hardships in order to provide staff (especially the non-malignant tumour cases) with an amicable departure. Without burning its bridges, the company may be able to re-employ some of these retrenched employees if it is able to reverse its fortune in the near future.

After the Retrenchment Process

After downsizing, communication will help to curb the negative effects and redirect the remaining employees' energies to their jobs. In this case, silence is not golden and sometimes is the worst policy. The staff should be told why such changes are necessary.   It is essential to win back trust after downsizing staff.

Reducing Fixed and Variable Overheads

Another effective way of cost control is to seek instant reductions in fixed and variable overheads. The turnaround CEO must exercise care not to cannibalize the entire operation – a surgical knife and not a *parang*[6] should be used here. Also, dramatic results can only be attained if cost reductions are done hand-in-hand with increase in sales and/or margins. Sometimes, cost reductions can be achieved through streamlining procedures and operations, by paring duplications and inefficient methodologies to the minimum.

In some instances, similar or more superior results are achieved through outsourcing. A company can literally outsource all its non-core functions today. Likewise, fixed overheads, especially people-related expenses can be reduced

---

[6] A long sword in the local context.

remarkably through cross-fertilization of multi-disciplinary skills. Productivity is improved by deploying staff to perform more value-added duties.

CASH FLOW

Money makes the world go round. Cash is king. Cash flow constitutes the lifeblood of a company and is a vital resource for ensuring its successful management and healthy operation. Skilful management of cash flow is even more acute and ranks above profitability in priority for small- and medium-size businesses. Sudden shortfall in cash flow will cause immediate massive difficulties. Cash flow management essentially requires the building up of the company's cash reserve, conserving and utilizing it wisely to maximize returns. Therefore, the approach should be two-pronged – boosting cash receipts and reducing cash outflows such as expenses (cost control). For a start, the turnaround CEO with the help of the accountant should review the company's profit and loss statements for the past three to six months or a longer period, if necessary, in order to obtain a fairly accurate picture of the company's loss in the average month. The goal is to bring the company back to a break-even or profitable position as soon as possible. It is imperative to plug any holes that are bleeding and avoid incurring further debts.

This last **C** Cash Flow is an indispensable ingredient in the turnaround plan, warranting the following measures:

Selling off unrelated businesses and non-core assets

One effective way to improve cash flow is to liquidate and sell off the company's non-core businesses and assets. Example of successful corporate turnaround after divesting its non-core assets and businesses is Neptune Orient Line (NOL). In 1997, NOL acquired APL, a leading shipping line. Shortly after, the Asian financial crisis struck, resulting in NOL's financial losses in 1997 and 1998. To address its financial woes, NOL took the bold steps of selling off its headquarters building, U.S. train network, and properties in several countries. NOL also closed its loss-making joint ventures in China. In 1999, NOL rebounded strongly when the Asian economy recovered. Another example is that of RBS. In 2010 Royal Bank of Scotland agreed to sell non-core asset management businesses worth $135 million to Aberdeen as it attempts to recover from a bruising financial crisis.

Controlling inventory level

Proper control of inventory is imperative as stocks not only tie up funds and add to carrying costs but they also rob the company of other investments or earning opportunities. The turnaround CEO must be mindful of the need to achieve an appropriate level of inventory. Miscalculations in the latter case can also be costly, resulting in stock-outs and lost sales, which may adversely affect the company's reliability and future business potential. Besides this, the turnaround CEO must also conduct a broad-based review of all the company's inventory items.

Reducing purchases/perks

By reducing purchases, the turnaround CEO is able to segregate those purchases that are absolutely essential (the must-have) for the smooth operations of the company from the superfluous (nice-to-have) ones. The underlying principle here is "look after the cents and the dollars will look after themselves." One such example is that of Mining Major Rio Tinto that in May 2009, engaged 12 Indian lawyers and is said to be increasing the number in order to help it bring down its approximately $100 million annual legal budget by 20 percent. Rio's managing attorney Leah Cooper said, "We took a look at our internal costs and the amount we were spending on outside counsel, and saw an opportunity to make significant changes." According to the company, since Indian lawyers are seven times cheaper than their counterparts in London, shifting part of the legal work to India from 1 May 2009 has already

2010 ' Corporate Turnaround Centre

brought savings of more than $1 million.

Reviewing and renegotiating terms

This involves a series of reviews and renegotiations covering a wide range of terms that may pose financial constraints for the cash-strapped company, including union terms, credit terms of suppliers and customers, as well as conditions for the use of banking facilities. The aim is to seek the most favourable terms, thereby boosting the cash flow and hopefully this will help jump-start the company's operations.

Union Terms

Dialogue with the labour union throughout the turnaround period is essential and should not be restricted to the retrenchment exercise. Proper communication with union leaders can serve several purposes, such as: (a) giving them an accurate outlook of the company so that they can prepare their members for what is to come; (b) garnering co-operation and support on implementation of unfavourable measures in order to save jobs, etc. The union and workers can be persuaded to co-operate if the management demonstrates its genuine effort to provide assistance and is concerned about their welfare. Of course, dialogues and negotiations must be conducted in a cordial and transparent manner.

Credit Terms

Account Payables

The goal is to hold on to cash as long as possible so that there is extra time to pay your company's bills. The credit terms of suppliers should be carefully studied to determine the best trade credit strategy.

Accounts Receivables

The company can also tap on its accounts receivables. During tough times, the company must exercise diligence in managing its account receivables. It is important to assign this important task to one of the turnaround team members for accountability. The turnaround CEO must ensure that collection activities are being monitored regularly and he must request that reports be given to him. In order to establish a successful collection program, the company needs to institute the following:

- Check references before granting credit.
- Establish credit terms in writing to customers.
- Send regular statements of accounts.
- Make calls on overdue accounts.
- Take legal action (where appropriate).

Rentals

Sometimes it is possible to negotiate with the landlord for temporary reduction in rental, rebates or even partial deferment in rentals to tide over the difficult period. Another alternative is to sublet the office premises, if there is a lot of empty space.

Banking Facilities

Credit lines should be drawn upon for emergencies. For short-term facilities such as overdrafts, the company can pay back a little amount from time to time. Quite often, tough negotiations with the "hospitals" (financial institutions or lenders) are also required to secure favourable terms to help tide the ailing company over during the difficult turnaround period.

EXERCISE 2.2

SURGICAL ACTION PLANNING – PART II

Continuing the action planning process, use the "surgical" processes related to cost control and cash flow to reorganize your company. Identify actions that must be taken, the individuals and/or departments that need to be involved, and determine the financial commitment required for each strategy.

	Key Steps	Actions	Individuals or Departments	Timeline	Costs or Savings
COST CONTROL	Cut operating budget				
	Downsize workforce				
	Reduce fixed and variable overheads				
CASH FLOW	Sell off unrelated businesses and non-core assets				
	Control inventory level				
	Reduce purchases/perks				
	Review and renegotiate terms				

2010 ' Corporate Turnaround Centre

Productivity Measurements for Phase 1

Productivity measurements generally are expressed as ratios and divide one number by another.

During this phase, financial and operational productivity are most important. As well, performance improvements are required, and required quickly. Monthly measurements should reveal whether the Phase 1 measures are effective.

Many of the standard management ratios apply to Phase 1. ROE, ROI and the Quick Ratio (Acid Test) are examples.

Other tests measure output against input. Here is just one set of examples derived from hourly manufacturing performance (HMP): hourly production outputs divided by hourly inputs. Exactly what should be measured as outputs and inputs is not so simple to decide:

- HMP in units/hour: Number of items produced divided by labour hours
- HMP (after defects) in units/hour: (Number of items produced minus number of defective items rejected) divided by labour hours
- HMP (labour) in $/$: Dollar value of items produced divided by labour costs
- HMP (all costs) in $/$: Dollar value of items produced divided by all costs (labour, materials, depreciation, energy, etc.)

At first, it may be important to compare your organization's productivity measurements against industry standards or your closest competitors. As Phase 1 continues, however, it will become more important to track improvements in the key metrics.

Phase 1 requires a life-saving surgical operation. The corporation may be heading for bankruptcy; drastic measures are being taken. Are the actions sufficient to save the organization?

During this phase, financial and operational productivity are most important. As well, performance improvements are required, and required quickly. Monthly measurements should reveal whether the Phase 1 measures are effective.

Here are some of the productivity measurements to take during this phase:

1. Savings per employee: Reductions in expenses (dollars) divided by the number of employees (headcount)
   - In the "Surgery" phase, staff turnover usually is desired: resignations will probably not be paired with new hires.
2. Profit ratio: Profits (dollars) divided by sales (dollars)
3. Staff turnover: Number of resignations divided by the number of employees (headcount)
   - In the Surgery phase, high turnover may be driven both by management downsizing the workforce and by employees leaving to avoid downsizing or layoffs. This may, therefore, reflect a deliberate cost-saving plan.
4. Return On Equity (**ROE**) is the familiar ratio: Return (profit after taxes) divided by shareholder equity
5. Employee sales performance (**ESP**): Sales (dollars) divided by the number of employees (headcount)
6. Sales to manufacturing performance: Number of product items sold divided by number of items produced
7. Hourly manufacturing performance (**HMP**): Number of items produced divided by number of hours of labour
   - This may either refer only to the direct factory labour, or to all staff including "overhead". With advances in computer-assisted design

and manufacturing (CAD and CAM), direct labour becomes smaller but "overhead" labour becomes larger – and possibly loses its meaning. Tracking and assigning costs for the labour to program each product's CAD and CAM may help distinguish profitable product lines from unprofitable ones.

8. Financial manufacturing performance (**FMP**): Number of items produced divided by cost of production (dollars)
9. Staff manufacturing performance: Number of items produced divided by the number of employees (headcount)
10. Sales manufacturing performance: Number of items produced divided by realized sales (dollars)
11. Profitable manufacturing performance: Number of items produced divided by realized (net) profit (dollars)
12. Revenue to wage performance (**RWP**): Corporate sales revenue (dollars) divided by total corporate wage cost (dollars)
13. Profit to wage performance (**PWP**): Net corporate profit (dollars) divided by total corporate wage cost (dollars)
14. Acid Test (Quick) Ratio is the familiar ratio: (Cash and equivalents plus marketable securities plus Accounts Receivable) divided by Current Liabilities
15. Hourly process performance: Number of items processed divided by number of hours of labour
    - This is the "process" brother to #7 above. How many cars are washed per employee-hour? How many clients are served per employee-week?
16. Return On Investment (**ROI**) is the familiar ratio: Return (profit after taxes) divided by the total new investment
17. Purchasing performance: Value of resources purchased divided by the cost of acquiring those resources
18. Cost-of-quality percentage: (Total cost of items produced minus cost of defective items produced) divided by total cost of items produced

19. Improvement in cost-of-quality percentage, based on the above percentage: (Current cost-of-quality percentage minus previous cost-of-quality percentage) divided by previous cost-of-quality percentage

20. Financial productivity performance: Improvement in a productivity measurement divided by the expense of the productivity initiatives (dollars)

21. Resource-based productivity performance: Improvement in a productivity measurement divided by the resources used in that production process

    - This is similar to "Technical energy performance" below. It relates more to the quantity of a resource than to the cost. As an example, if a technically-better paint "does the job" in one coat rather than two, this index would double. An increase in the unit cost of the paint might be offset by reduced storage and labour costs; but this performance metric is strictly based on quantity or volume, rather than cost.

22. Financial energy performance (**FEP**): Number of items produced divided by the cost of the energy required (dollars)

23. Technical energy performance (**TEP**): Number of items produced divided by the energy required (KW of electricity or litres of fuel, etc.)

24. Return On Invested Capital (**ROIC**) is the familiar ratio: Return (profit after taxes) divided by the total invested capital (total assets minus both uninvested cash and non-interest-bearing current liabilities)

25. Change in employee sales performance (**ESP**) from #5 above: Current ESP minus previous ESP

26. Change in hourly manufacturing performance (**HMP**) from #7 above: Current HMP minus previous HMP

27. Change in financial manufacturing performance (**FMP**) from #8 above: Current FMP minus previous FMP

28. Change in revenue to wage performance (**RWP**) from #12 above: Current FWP minus previous FWP

29. Change in profit to wage performance (**PWP**) from #13 above: Current PWP minus previous PWP

30. Change in financial energy performance (**FEP**) from #21 above: Current FEP minus previous FEP

The surgery is over and the patient is about to come around. You have applied the **four Cs** of Communication, Concentration, Cost Control and Cash Flow and you have made your plans based on productivity measurments. You are now ready for Resuscitation, the first part of which is featured in the next module.

END OF MODULE #2 Remember the 4 Cs in corporate restructuring: Concentration, Communication, Cost-cutting and Cash Flow. Use the productivity measurements appropriate to your corporation to prepare to resuscitate it.

Additional Online Resources

The following books authored by Dr. Mike Teng are relevant to module #2, and cover the Surgery Phase. Details are available by clicking on the website below for each book.

Corporate Turnaround: Global perspective

www.turnaroundguru.com

A study of the various corporate turnaround techniques used all around the world, e.g., China, Russia, Europe, Latin America, etc.

Corporate Turnaround: Nursing a sick company back to health (Second Edition)

www.michaelteng.com

Following the success of the first edition which was a best-selling book in 2002, Dr Michael Teng revised the book to incorporate new strategies to handle new challenges facing the modern day corporations. Do not miss reading this book for the second time as it crystallizes some of the best-kept secrets in corporate turnaround and transformation

You can also visit Dr. Mike Teng's www.youtube.com/1103teng **to watch the YouTube videos of some of the books.**

Corporate Turnaround to save company

http://tinyurl.com/corporateturnaround1

Sub-prime crisis, Bear Stearns, Freddie Mac, Fannie Mae, Lehman Brothers, AIG, Washington Mutual, Bradford & Bingley and Fortis. Governmental financial rescue, global recession: crisis after crisis. Will there be a Second Depression? What is next? For sure, all companies need to go through corporate turnaround to save them or transform them in the new landscape.

Corporate Transformation Centre - Corporate Hospital

http://tinyurl.com/corporatetransformationcentre

When you are sick, you visit a doctor for treatment. When you have cancer, you do not even visit the general practitioner, you visit an oncologist or cancer specialist. Yet, many sick companies do not seek help early enough. Similar to physical health, the key in a successful transformation is early diagnosis and treatment. Also, these sick companies do not know where to seek help for corporate turnaround. This is the rationale for setting up a corporate hospital or corporate transformation centre (CTC).

Corporate turnaround management for prosperity

http://tinyurl.com/corporateturnaround

There are many so-called corporate viruses that can affect the health of your company. The rapid changes of globalization, and the slowdown that the global economy is now experiencing at a scary rate, are examples of corporate viruses. In addition to this, incompetent management is a very serious cause for the lack of growth or the sickness of your company. Corporate Turnaround is the best solution. Recession is a part of the macroeconomic cycle. Therefore, it occurs after a certain period, but this time it is not a usual recession. The on-going recession is equivalent to the great Depression of the 1930s. This is the greatest virus that companies have encountered since World War II. Therefore, companies around the world have to take immediate measures to save themselves and do a corporate turnaround immediately.

MODULE #3

–

PHASE TWO:

RESUSCITATION

Part I

2010 ' Corporate Turnaround Centre

WHAT IS THE RESUSCITATION PHASE?

Surgery alone is not sufficient to turn around a company. After the detailed repair of an ailment, the patient must then be resuscitated and given therapy in order to fully regain health and become even stronger than before the ailment occurred.

The role of the turnaround manager is also to grow the business. There is always a limit to a cost-cutting exercise, which is more short term. Growing the business is critical to sustain recovery. This is why Mehrdad Baghai, *et al.,* said: *"Successful companies must grow new businesses: that is what leads to sustained profitable growth."* Companies are like living organisms that need to grow; otherwise they will wither and die. The mandatory requirements to staying in business today are possessing good-quality products and services, and using high technology. These are pre-requisites and "givens" for your participation in the industry. Hence, in this chapter, the resuscitation techniques are more marketing-oriented.

The resuscitation regime consists of first trying to determine the corporate objectives and direction. Next, the turnaround CEO has to gather market information by being on the ground to personally evaluate the information gathered from the marketplace. In some cases, the use of external help to verify one's own finding is useful. The marketplace here refers to focusing on the developments of customers as well as competitors. The turnaround CEO can then direct his attention to implementing short-term strategies in product, price as well as marketing. In the longer term, to fully resuscitate the company, the turnaround CEO has to devise plans to differentiate his products/services using service and quality to strengthen the company's brand name and invest in future expansions. In summary, the resuscitation phase to grow the business involves the following steps:

1. Ascertaining corporate objectives
2. Staying on the ground/using consultants (if necessary)
3. Developing the right product and price
4. Implementing an aggressive marketing strategy
5. Differentiating using service quality
6. Strengthening the brand name
7. Investing in future expansions

This module will focus on the first four steps; the remainder are covered in module #5.

ASCERTAINING CORPORATE OBJECTIVES

This part of the turnaround process requires the formulation and crystallization of the company's corporate objectives. This step is essential, as once the corporate objectives are clearly defined, they serve to steer the company towards the direction it should be heading. The company will not be easily side-tracked or distracted and every employee will be heading towards common goals. To be achievable, corporate objectives require active control over the company's finances, as well as the unwavering support of the company's stakeholders, such as shareholders, business associates and staff. Otherwise, the turnaround CEO will face an uphill if not impossible task.

The greater a company's ability to control costs in relation to its revenues, the more its earnings power is enhanced. Some common procedures and concepts iterated in the Surgery phase (Phase I), such as zero-based budgeting and control margins of projects, can also be applied here to control finances. Once key corporate objective issues are resolved, staff members are no longer in limbo but can move full steam ahead towards achieving the corporate objectives. Action is demanded, not just empty words.

STAYING ON THE GROUND / USING CONSULTANTS (IF NECESSARY)

Once the corporate objectives are in place, the turnaround CEO needs to gather information to make wise decisions. He can make use of external consultants but must be personally on the ground to verify the information. External consultants – like therapists – do have a role to play in helping companies understand the strategies to venture into new markets and products, mergers and acquisitions (M&A), promotion of brand names, etc. They can be a valuable resource during the resuscitation phase, as consultants can provide other insights and perspectives to give the business a new booster shot.

However, one cannot depend totally on external consultants. At this stage, it is also imperative that the turnaround CEO keep his ears and eyes on the ground. Nowadays, this is often substituted with the easier option of engaging external consultants to do the total job. Besides being more costly, this alternative may compromise some of the benefits of better decision-making. This is because sometimes recommendations made from a third-party perspective could be distorted and rather different from the "ground-level" viewpoint.

There is an increasing trend in the engagements of external consultants by some companies for the wrong reasons. This is probably spurred on for political reasons. Instead of approaching their board of management directly with their own recommendations, the management of some companies tend to make use of external consultants as spin doctors to engineer the desired recommendations, which are then presented to their board members in a more palatable and highly professional manner. In this way, there is a higher chance

2010 ' Corporate Turnaround Centre

of the desired recommendations being accepted by the board of management. Should your company decide to engage an external turnaround consultant after weighing the pros and cons, then you need to be clear on the scope of assistance required. The choice of a good consultant is a critical one and you should do your homework and take time to consider carefully before signing on the dotted line.

It is useful to conduct preliminary talks with at least three potential consultant candidates in order to obtain general information about their backgrounds, areas of specialisation and other relevant information. During such informal discussions, it is useful to discuss your company's requirements on a general basis to assess broadly the problem-solving skills offered by each of these candidates. Thereafter, you can conduct interviews for more in-depth understanding of each consultant's personal background, forté, consulting experience, general business philosophy, and so forth. As close rapport is required, the existence of compatible chemistry is crucial. Reference checks are also mandatory, as these are excellent sources of feedback on actual assignments done by the consultants. Once the choice of consultant is finalised, you must agree with the consultant on terms such as time-frame required, cost, and definition of scope of work rendered. To avoid future dispute, all these should be documented.

Sun Tzu was truly an advocate of the "staying on the ground" policy when he remarked: "Generally, in the case of armies you wish to strike, cities you wish to attack, and people you wish to assassinate, you must know the names of the garrison commander, the staff officers, the ushers, gate keepers and the bodyguards. You must instruct your agents to inquire into these matters in minute detail." In order to stay on the ground, the turnaround CEO must talk to various people – staff, suppliers, customers, business partners and even competitors. Through these various channels, the turnaround CEO is able to acquire better knowledge of the industry. In addition, he may be able to get a better feel of the market conditions, whether local, regional or worldwide. By

2010' Corporate Turnaround Centre

staying on the ground, the turnaround CEO does not operate in a vacuum and is better equipped to make sound decisions and take timely action. This will not only check or halt declining trends but hopefully improve them in the near future.

RIGHT PRODUCT AND PRICE

After determining all the relevant information, the turnaround CEO should next consider the launch of the right product and price to resuscitate the business.

Right Product

Although many products are labelled as "new" and "improved", they are actually not new breeds; they are mongrels. And while they may be different in some trivial way, they are hardly improved. Instead of exciting customers, many will fail in the marketplace because they are merely repackaged and reformulated. What perks customers up is product leadership, a company displaying the ability and determination to make products recognised as superior – products that deliver real benefit and performance improvements.

Product leaders are aware that customers have a much broader perception of performance apart from the utilitarian benefits. These customers expect the performance breakthrough products that can move their rational and emotional selves.

Indeed, for some products/services, experiential or emotional impact is a prime measure of performance: Nike, Reebok and Swatch products indulge people's hunger for an association with sports heroes, the rich and famous or peer recognition – in the same way that Revlon sells hope, not cosmetics.

Take Microsoft's Xbox, for example. Moving into the gaming arena was a daring

2010 ' Corporate Turnaround Centre

move when the company introduced its game console in 2001; a year after Sony's PlayStation 2 hit the market. But Microsoft believed it had the marketing and distribution strengths as well as the brand awareness to enable it to win in this market. Though the Xbox still has only a fraction of PlayStation 2's installed base, it did manage to outsell PlayStation 2 for the first time during the last quarter of 2004, signalling that Microsoft did not overshoot its capabilities in this space.

Right Price

Getting a good price for your product is similar to a good mouth-to-mouth resuscitation, it is easy to administer without much hassle (unlike some other plans that may require more investments). Yet, it can yield immediate results for the bottom-line if done correctly. Make sure you clearly examined your strengths and weaknesses in getting a good price. It is rather common for companies selling to Asian markets to encounter the following problem: Their high-margin, good-quality products which are the rage in the United States and Europe, cannot fetch a high price here. Why? Developing the right product does not always guarantee success in this part of the world, as markets here are heavily biased towards pricing. This is what my mother would term the "cheap and good" mentality which is highly prevalent in Asia. Mothers always know best. Therefore, in order to penetrate the Asian market, companies must not neglect the right pricing for their products.

Johnson & Johnson, for example, grew the capabilities of its core business in contact lenses over time. First it acquired a small contact-lens manufacturer, then improved production processes and efficiencies by licensing new technologies and by effectively using vendors to cut costs. With that capability-building process behind it, Johnson & Johnson could then more confidently commit the resources to a new business – disposable contact lenses – which has become a very profitable part of its portfolio.

In the context of management theory, it is useful to apply the best blend of Eastern and Western practices. Developing Asia can learn much from the more established and intellectual Western managerial professionalism in the area of clear vision, proper research and feedback. The financial crisis has exposed the weakness of some mega-corporation in the East. For instance a number of Chaebols[7] in Korea and Keiretsu in Japan collapsed or had to face tough times. They were lacking in focus, over-extended and diversified. Their product lines had little connections with each other. On the other hand, the top blue chip companies in the West such as Microsoft, Coca-Cola (a/k/a Coke), and IBM were mainly one-product companies with a clear and focused corporate vision. During that era, companies like Apple displayed this unified vision through the underlying theme running throughout their products that is even evident today in the marketplace. But you can look to the more recent economic downturn and see that vision is simply not enough. Lack of prudence and strategy caused the collapse of Lehman Brothers and the subsequent collapse of many banks plunging the world into a recession. Vision alone is not enough.

Cmbinating all three elements will lead to a successful company.

The West can learn from Asia's entrepreneurs' acumen and instincts to quickly act on the information available. The Japanese have taught the West about quick implementation of quality systems and products and concepts like Just-in-Time which is only now reaching deeper into the U.S. to penetrate markets in the South and Central American regions. Now the Chinese and the Indians are winning the fight against the Japanese corporations in the areas of low-cost and good-quality products and services. Therefore, to compete effectively in today's global marketplace, it is vital to integrate the vision and feedback management system of the West with the entrepreneurial and intuitive action of the East.

---

[7] Chaebol refers to a South Korean form of business conglomerate.

AGGRESSIVE MARKETING STRATEGY

For revitalisation efforts to succeed during the turnaround period, the turnaround CEO needs to implement an aggressive marketing strategy. This strategy can be applied to resuscitate and jump-start the company's failing health, much like the way electro-cardiopulmonary resuscitation (CPR using shock paddles) is administered to a patient whose vital signs are fading. The aggressive marketing strategy may include penetrating new markets, inventing and launching a product, renting out a building that is causing financial strain or even merely announcing a major price increase to customers. However, the right resuscitation strategy or medicine has to be applied; otherwise you may kill the patient.

An ineffective marketing strategy is like an aphrodisiac; it excites you for a short while but does not solve your impotence.

The first victims in the company's bid to drastically reduce costs are usually the marketing and public relations personnel. This is because their presence constitutes non-essential expenditures during downturns. However, as marketing staff can be considered the arms and legs of the company, measures to cut back on these would further damage the company's sales potential. Hence, during hard times, the company should endeavour to increase sales but not reduce its sales force, marketing budget and related expenses. During bad times, you need more business, not less. In fact, it would be lovely to poach your competitors' sales personnel if they are retrenched, as they can provide you with an invaluable source of market intelligence on the competitors' customer base, pricing, and other highly sensitive information. Likewise, your competitors would love to poach your good sales staff.

2010 ' Corporate Turnaround Centre

As Sun Tzu said "… It is only the enlightened ruler and the wise general who will use the highest intelligence of the army for purposes of spying and thereby achieve great results. Spies are the most important element … because on them depends an army's ability to move."

In the midst of difficulties, sometimes the perception of the problems makes them seem larger than they actually are. There is also a tendency for the staff to wallow in self-pity, licking their own wounds or playing the game of shame and blame. They may place blame on everything conceivable – the competition is too intense, the customers are too demanding, the former bosses did not do a good job and so on. The situation becomes like this: "We have met the enemies and they are us!" This could be said for the current global credit crisis. This depression is a key example that, if we look back and identify the real issues, can be used to change the banking system and put in new rules and regulations and prevent the same mistakes from occurring in the future.

Finally, another area often neglected during the turnaround period is the use of computer technology to garner more sales or new business. Of particular interest is e-commerce, which is here to stay. The big incentive of venturing into e-commerce is to make profits and stay in business.

Online Marketing Strategy

All successful online marketers also say the same thing. Aggressive marketing is good marketing.

You have to make sure you put the right things in front of the right people, and that you give them a chance to absorb it. A person might not get all your messages because they're busy or they were interrupted while reading it. Maybe they're waiting for a specific day to make purchases? Your job is giving reminders. Give them a chance to see your product.

Aggressive marketing also means marketing your product in as many ways as possible. Every little bit of effort counts. It's like a snowball effect. You start off with small contributions here and there, but after 3 months, you'll have a huge snowball.

Use free classifieds, solo ads, pay-per-clicks, write articles for submissions, social networking sites, traffic exchanges, basically whatever you can get your hands on!

Not only are you getting your product out there, but you're also getting yourself out there! Think about what writing articles and publishing them over the Internet could do. If someone recognizes you several times in several different places, they'll decide that you're busy with your business and that you must be doing something right. This will only help increase your credibility.

For more on maximising your use of the Internet, see Module #4, covering Ultimate Internet Marketing.

"Closing the gate"

Shout it from the roof tops, shout it from the schools
That you have to use the Web, or you'll be a fool
There is no way forward other than using our brains
There is only stagnation, and nasty, horrible pain

The world is travelling on a bumpy, economic slide
The world is unravelling; don't get lost on the ride
Tell the students in universities, and big business owners
We have to utilise the Web, because there are no money donors

The waves are crashing, and breaking against the shore,
You do not seem convinced; let me tell you some more,
The Web has influence and power like the force in Star Wars
The Web can give you riches; just don't get drunk in bars

For you are wasting your time trying to think like the old days
You need to restructure your lines and think into ways that pay
New ways of marketing will get your message heard,
Don't be fooled by security; don't get lost with the herd

You're better than you think you are. You're better than the pack
But you can't get lazy or crazy; you have to pick up the slack
The world waits for no man, so get killer copy writing,
The world waits for no woman, and this is where it gets exciting

Credibility is everything; targeting traffic the ideal
Professional websites and passion will keep things real
Making money this way will pull us out of this recession
Making money like this will stop us reverting in regression

2010 ' Corporate Turnaround Centre

130

So teach this to the students, teach this to all the kids:
That using these methods will stop us hitting the skids
New ways of working have to be respected and learned,
The new ways of working will stop us getting burned.

So get a good quality product and sell it to the masses,
Before we're out of a job and the stock market crashes,
If we act now before it's too late, we can avoid a fate
Where we have no work as someone has closed the gate.

EXERCISE 3.1

RESUSCITATING YOUR COMPANY, PART I

To focus your attention on resuscitation and the contents of this module, consider the following questions in relation to your company.

1. **Do you have crystal-clear corporate objectives? If not, what should they be? If so, are they still fit for the future?**

2. **What have you done lately, as the Turnaround CEO, to "stay on the ground"?**

3. **Do you have the right product at the right price for the market?**

4. **How have you aligned your marketing strategy to the future?**

2010' Corporate Turnaround Centre

Productivity Measurements for Phase 2 Part 1

This phase introduces several new priorities: setting short-term objectives in light of market opportunities, the competitive environment; and laying the foundation for growth. Future growth will depend on quality, brand-strength, and investing in new opportunities.

The standard test for quality involves a ratio comparing non-defective products to all products. With these measurements, "100% quality" means that no defects were detected. Here is just one set of examples derived from manufacturing quality percentages (MQP):

- MQP (item count): (Total number of items produced minus number of defective items produced) divided by total number of items produced
- MQP ($/$):(Total dollar value of items produced minus value of defective items produced) divided by total value of items produced
- MQP (labour hours): (Total labour hours spent to produce the items minus the sum of initial and rework hours for defective items) divided by total labour hours

At first, it may be important to compare your organization's productivity measurements against industry standards or your closest competitors. As Phase 1 continues, however, it will become more important to track improvements in the key metrics.

This phase introduces several new priorities:

- Determine objectives, noting market opportunities and competitor's positions
- Make short-term changes in product mix, pricing and marketing
- Lay the foundations for growth by improving quality, strengthening the brand, and investing in new business opportunities.

Quality may be measured as a percentage of non-defective products relative to all products. This may be measured on different metrics: number of units, cost of inputs, or value of outputs.

Brand-strength may be measured as the premium a customer is willing to pay for the desired brand over a similar product from another brand. Ideally, this premium will be calculated after all discounts and rebates have been considered. If prices are reduced during the surgery and resuscitation phases (to move old inventory or to maintain cash flow), there may not be a measurable improvement until the third stage.

Here are some of the productivity measurements to take during this phase:

1. Savings per employee: Reduction in expenses (dollars) divided by the number of employees (head count)
2. Financial productivity performance: Improvement in a productivity measurement divided by the expense of the productivity initiatives (dollars)
3. Gains in revenue per product line: Within each product line, divide the most recent annual sales revenue (dollars) by the previous annual sales revenue (dollars)
4. Gains in profit per product line: Within each product line, divide the most recent annual profit (dollars) by the previous annual profit (dollars)
5. Employee sales performance: Sales (dollars) divided by the number of employees (head count)
6. Sales to manufacturing performance: Number of product items sold divided by number of items produced
7. Manufacturing quality percentage by item count: (Total number of items produced minus number of defective items produced) divided by total number of items produced

8. Improvement in manufacturing quality percentage based on the above percentage: (Current manufacturing quality percentage minus previous manufacturing quality percentage) divided by previous manufacturing quality percentage

9. Value-of-quality percentage: (Total value of items produced minus lost value of defective items produced) divided by total value of items produced

10. Improvement in value-of-quality percentage, based on the above percentage: (Current value-of-quality percentage minus previous value-of-quality percentage) divided by previous value-of-quality percentage

11. Quality control effectiveness (**QCE**) by item count: Number of defective items caught by internal controls divided by (number of defective items caught by internal controls plus number of defective items caught by customers)

12. Improvement in QCE by item count, based on the above percentage: (Current QCE by item count minus previous QCE by item count) divided by previous QCE by item count

13. Quality control effectiveness (**QCE**) by cost: Cost of defective items caught by internal controls divided by (cost of defective items caught by internal controls plus cost of defective items caught by customers)

14. Improvement in QCE by cost, based on the above percentage: (Current QCE by cost minus previous QCE by cost) divided by previous QCE by cost

15. Quality control effectiveness (**QCE**) by value: Value of defective items caught by internal controls divided by (value of defective items caught by internal controls plus value of defective items caught by customers)

16. Improvement in QCE by value, based on the above percentage: (Current QCE by value – previous QCE by value) divided by previous QCE by value

17. Brand strength by product line (**BSPL**): Within each product line, divide (our selling price minus industry average selling price) by industry average selling price

18. Improvement in brand strength by product line, based on the above metric: (Current BSPL minus previous BSPL) divided by previous BSPL

19. Percentage growth in business opportunities by count: (Current number of opportunities minus previous number of opportunities) divided by previous number of opportunities

20. Percentage growth in business opportunities by investment, measured in dollars: (Current investment in opportunities minus previous investment in opportunities) divided by previous investment in opportunities

21. Percentage growth in business opportunities by revenue, measured in dollars: (Current revenue from opportunities minus previous revenue from opportunities) divided by previous revenue from opportunities

22. Percentage growth in business opportunities by profit, measured in dollars: (Current profit from opportunities minus previous profit from opportunities) divided by previous profit from opportunities

23. Delay in approving (or rejecting) the pursuit of new innovations: Average number of days elapsed from the suggestion of a new innovation to the time it is rejected or approved for formal research.

24. Delay in approving (or rejecting) spending $1,000 in the pursuit of new innovations: Average number of days elapsed from the suggestion of a new innovation to the time it is rejected or approved for formal research, per $1,000.
    a. Depending on the organization, the dollar amount could be different: $100,000 or $1,000,000 might be reasonable for a large corporation
    b. The key concept for these "delay" metrics is that the company should not vacillate in choosing whether or not to pursue an opportunity

25. Percent reduction in the delay for approving or rejecting spending $1,000 on innovations (**DASI**): (Current DASI minus previous DASI) divided by previous DASI

26. Percentage of revenue spent for marketing (advertising) (**PRSM**): Cost of marketing (in dollars) divided by total revenue (in dollars)

27. Change in the percentage of revenue spent for marketing: Current PRSM minus previous PRSM

28. Growth of the percentage of revenue spent for marketing: (Current PRSM minus previous PRSM) divided by the previous PRSM

29. Percentage of revenue spent on new product innovation (market research, technical research and development, planning marketing strategies, etc.) (**PCSI**): Cost of innovation (in dollars) divided by total revenue (in dollars)

30. Percentage of revenue spent to train and motivate sales and marketing personnel (**PRTS**): Cost of training and motivating the sales and marketing staff (including regional meetings and incentive programs) (in dollars) divided by total revenue (in dollars)

2010 ' Corporate Turnaround Centre

END OF MODULE #3

The patient is beginning to revitalize. You have clear objectives, your feet firmly on the ground and the right product at the right price. Aggression in marketing is the next priority for your company and the next module looks at online marketing and how to make sure you are ahead of the competition.

~

2010 ' Corporate Turnaround Centre

Additional Online Resources

The following books authored by Dr. Mike Teng are relevant to modules #3 and #5, covering the Resuscitation Phase. Details are available by clicking on the website below for each book.

Fundamentals of Buying and Selling of Companies

www.restructuringspecialist.com

This book is written in a simple and easy-to-understand manner on the complex topic of mergers and acquisitions and what to do look for when buying and selling companies.

Buying and Selling of Distressed Companies

www.restructuringexpert.com

Investing in distressed assets can prove to be very profitable, as they are at rock bottom prices. This book delves into the nitty-gritty of what to look for when identifying such gems.

Post-Merger Integration

www.changemanagementorganizational.com

Shareholders' values are often marginalised after a merger or acquisition. This is because companies that merge only look at the strategic and financial, but they fail to take care of the post-merger integration issues, such as cultural fit.

You can also visit Dr. Mike Teng's www.youtube.com/1103teng **to watch the YouTube videos of some of his books.**

Beware of the Merger

http://tinyurl.com/bewareofmerger

Merger is a good corporate turnaround and transformation strategy. However, the majority of mergers do not add value to the shareholders. This is because

2010 ' Corporate Turnaround Centre

companies merge for all the wrong reasons: ego reasons with no homework done. CEOs find it quicker and more glamorous to grow by merging rather than by organic growth. They fail to integrate the stakeholders and the organizations properly, thus it results in failure.

Post-Merger Integration

http://tinyurl.com/postmerger

Shareholders' values are often marginalised after a merger or acquisition. This video reminds us of companies that merge only looking at the pre-merger issues, e.g., strategic and financial, which are more exciting. They fail to take care of post-merger integration issues such as cultural fit.

Going for public listing

http://tinyurl.com/publiclisting

Many SMEs want to go for public listing so that the founders can make their money and retire. However, these founders need to make sure that their companies are ready. The corporate governance and compliance are getting very tight and strict in many jurisdictions. There are advantages with public listing such as making the profile of the firm more visible. Outsiders feel more comfortable dealing with listed company as its financial reporting is more transparent. Insiders also feel proud working for a listed firm.

Buying a company

http://tinyurl.com/buyingacompany

Everyone wants to be his or her own boss. The easiest way to do this is to have your own business. You can own a business and be your own boss. But to own a business, you either need to start your own business or buy an existing one. Starting a business is not for everyone but yes, just about anyone and everyone can buy an existing business.

Buying distressed companies

http://tinyurl.com/distressedassets

Distressed securities include stocks, bonds or other financial claims of companies that are close to or have reached financial distress. If a company has filed for bankruptcy, it is under financial distress. This category also includes bank debt and non-performing loans. They fail to make regular interest or principal payments, and they trade at yields higher than those of similar dated treasuries. Once their financial distress becomes evident, there is panic selling and they then trade at deep discounts. At this stage, they present an attractive opportunity to anyone who has analyzed their true worth. In recent years, private firms such as hedge funds and private equity firms have been among the largest buyers of distressed securities. They hold the securities until they have appreciated.

MODULE #4

ULTIMATE INTERNET MARKETING: FOCUS ON PRODUCTIVITY & INNOVATION

"Time to find a new way"
(Ultimate Internet strategy)

It is hard to envision working from home
It is hard to enlighten people that feel alone
It's time for change, time to tell the people
Time to think fresh, time to stop being feeble

There are opportunities, to make money from home
There are ways to market, our companies that set the tone
The world is in turmoil, and this has affected our economy
The world is in disarray, and put our future in jeopardy

Chorus
It's time to tell the message, to all our pupils
It's time to spread the message, like the disciples
Time to teach the new ways that will secure our future
Time to teach the new methods to the young and mature

Affiliate programs and quality, should be taught in our schools
Killer sales copy and marketing will stop us looking like fools
Sincere passion and domains will help us avoid economic pain,
With no work or money, sooner or later you will go insane,

You need to be patient and persistent, you must never give in
Through the bad times and hard times, to quit would be a sin
It's just a question of sticking with it, and trying your best
To help you persevere and get through it, think of it as test

Chorus

It's time to tell the message to all our pupils

It's time to spread the message like the disciples

Time to teach the new ways that will secure our future

Time to teach the new methods to the young and mature

University students should be well versed in the ways of the Web,

University students should know all there is in the ways to get ahead,

For the good times will only roll if our children know all there is,

About using the Web for working from home and doing the biz,

The old business methods are not as good as they used to be,

The old business ways have to move over - it is plain to see,

Overheads such as rental costs do not need to be considered,

If the Internet home market is used and properly configured,

Chorus

It's time to tell the message to all our pupils

It's time to spread the message like the disciples

Time to teach the new ways that will secure our future

Time to teach the new methods to the young and mature

INTRODUCTION

Today, the Internet has paved the way for an entirely new universe full of opportunities for even the most insignificant business owner who is home-based. There are many successful self-made millionaires who utilized Internet intelligently to achieve success. The newly minted rich are no different than we.

They began their Internet companies from the ground floor, found a niche for themselves and meticulously worked on to achieve success.

KEY FACTORS FOR INTERNET MARKETING SUCCESS

If you are under the impression that you can jump in, create a website, submit it to a few directories or blogs, sit down, relax and watch those thousands of dollars come in, then you are not heading in the right direction. It's not going to happen. You need to really think: Who are you and where do you want to be in the future? Whether offline or online, there are only two things that matter: "Buying" and "Selling". Basically, to simplify, it all comes down to this:

Know your customer
What is he or she specifically looking for? You must know their problems or their desires. You must be in their shoes and find out what would make them feel better, then make an offer.

What do you offer?
Why should they buy from you? How come you're better than the rest? Why should they trust you? Are you offering your own or someone else's product? How will you create an irresistible offer so they will beg you to sell it to them?

Some Key Success Factors are:

A True and Sincere Zeal

To succeed, you need passion for your business. If you lack true passion, you cannot achieve the success you are looking for.

Your Personal Domain

(For example: www.yourspecificdomain.com)

If you host your business using a free server it is rarely taken seriously. They tend to be thought of as unprofessional. A company that does not care enough for an exclusive domain name might not be able to attract customers who would feel confident about doing business there. A company having an exclusive domain name and a professional-looking website is likely to have a significantly higher success rate compared to the majority of business sites that are hosted using free servers.

Professional Website

Your site is a direct reflection of your attitude, personality, and the business you have created. Designing a professional-looking site with a purpose of making sales takes a great deal of effort and time, seeing that there are other factors beyond the design of the website. You need to look at the big picture and intentionally design your website to sell.

Informative, Good Quality Content

If you wish to create a constant flow of traffic, you need to give your visitors something that would attract them to return to your site frequently. Just one visit is not enough to maintain a business. You need to keep your visitors informed and entertained with new content on a regular basis.

It is very clear that it is the art of writing that matters. If you have been successful at optimizing your content then it is obvious that you can gain great rewards from the visitors. You will make enormous profits if the article written is good enough to drag the search engine directories toward your site, hence making people opt for you first.

Focused and Targeted Traffic

Regardless of how good your website is, if you are not getting high-quality, authentic traffic you cannot succeed. Your website could get 'x' number of visitors each day; but if none of them is interested in the service or products that you offer, your web traffic is useless. You have to encourage and receive continual, targeted traffic on your website. Create something of value that people will pass around. It can be a report with useful information that you allow people to give away. It can also be some kind of cool and unusual webpage that people will want to e-mail to all their friends. Of course, the pass-around item will include your advertisement and your link, spreading the word about your website. This is a "viral" strategy.

Opt-in List (Ezine)

Creating your personally designed publication is essential for success. This provides direct contact with probable customers and will also allow you to sponsor goods and services as well as create credibility.

Your Own In-Demand Product

Marketing affiliate programs might provide good income, but the real profits come from marketing a product of your own that you know is in demand.

Killer Sales Copy

We know pens are mightier than swords! The words you create are the reflection of your personality. The product, design of the website and well-planned marketing strategies all hinge on what you have to say. You should

XXXX ' Corporate Turnaround Centre

know how to write a sales letter that can persuade your desired customers. You need to empathize with your customers' needs. This will direct you to create the letter with passion, enthusiasm, and advantage.

Killer Marketing Strategy

Creating a killer strategy is vital for the success of your online business. To succeed, you will have to develop and follow a strategy throughout that would include the following:

- A great product
- A website specifically developed to sell the product or
- service
- A fool-proof marketing strategy

And, remember, all these together can ensure your SUCCESS!

Instantaneous Product Delivery

Ensure fast download, instant access, and easy navigation with a simple "look" and online payment options.

People surf the Internet to find information. The users wish to find what they are looking for. The best products for the buyer on the Internet are the ones that are delivered instantly.

Accept Credit Cards

When you conduct business over the Internet, it is imperative that you accept credit cards. You need to provide visitors with a simple online ordering process that they can follow, with the convenience to pay for their order online. You could also set up an account with a third party such as PayPal.

Developing Credibility

For an Internet-based entrepreneur, it is important to ensure that his or her visitors feel comfortable with the vendor and with the website. So, to get your visitor's confidence and trust, you have to build your credibility. Your attitude is a pivotal factor in shaping your success. You need to remain optimistic and be always ready to face any challenge that you might have along the way. The truth is that you are able do whatever you please. You just need to believe that 'you can' and most importantly, 'believe in yourself'.

Presence

Classified ads could determine your success. There is no reason to belittle this option. A majority of people spend considerable time offline and you must utilize this time. If you have a physical presence or location, make sure you do the following:

- Put out signs that attract users. The words that lead most of the users are "Find us here....on the Internet" and the ideal search engine friendly URL will be "www.myspecificdomain.com".
- Have a catalogue available online that helps the customer to look and shop.
- Print your email address and website on everything: brochures, business cards, cash register tape, invoices, letterhead, packing lists, and other related publicity options.
- If you are the first business in your specific area or field to establish an online presence, it is simple to publish an article in your local newspaper to inform the general public about it. Be in touch with the newspaper that covers stories on new businesses. If you find the right person/correspondent at the local trade magazine, you could publish a write-up on your business.
- Disburse press releases to your local magazines that you think that are read by your target audience. If your business is featured in the "what's new" column you will be able attract local users' attention.
- If you can gather the funds, keep a computer in your store. You coudl also consider putting up a booth at a trade show to allow your customers to visit your site.

Set up a virtual tour of your business on your website.

If you have the email addresses of your buyers, you can send them emails announcing a special offering or sale, or to just remind them of your shop and business. If you have customers without an email address, you can fax or post a monthly newsletter that lists items that are for sale.

Producing virtual tours for clients who are seeking the ultimate marketing tool for their websites has the potential to generate profits far in excess. Virtual tours can range from a hotel that gives potential guests a tour of their facility, accommodations and amenities via their website, to real estate brokers that broadcast house tours of properties they have listed for sale and posted on their websites. To get started, you'll need specialized software, a computer and a digital camcorder, not to mention production and editing skills to produce the finished product. Marketing the service can be as easy as creating a few sample virtual tours and posting the tours on your own website for potential clients to view, as well as hiring a direct sales force to solicit business.

MARKET ANALYSIS

Market analysis is the basis of the marketing plan. Each plan must ideally include a very simple and comprehensible explanation of the segmentation of the market, a forecast for the market, and a focus on the target market.

Essential Market Analysis

If you want to devise a feasible plan on the basis of the dispositions and needs of your consumers, you will have to find the answers to the following questions outlined below:

- Who are these people?
- Where are they?
- What do they want out of this relationship?

- What method(s) do they use to make their buying decisions?
- At what stores do they shop?
- How do you send your messages in sales and marketing?

You must know the answers to these questions regardless of who your potential customers are. This also hold true when a non-profit organization goes into a market looking for funding, in-kind contributions and volunteer participation. The research relevant to this market analysis will start with data that provides a complete count of businesses, classrooms, households, and workers in a market. These are basic demographics. What you will require depends on whether you're targeting businesses, households, or individuals. Whenever you can, you should separate households by income level, businesses by size, and workers by job type, education, and other factors.

Employment statistics bring in additional information on the background and education of workers. Another way to separate your target customers is by psychographics.

CONCLUSION

Although there are many ways that you can obtain free promotion and advertising on the Internet, in order to be successful, you must be willing to invest in your business.

Investing in your business will include your time, purchasing advertising, services, software or whatever it takes to help your business profit.

If you look at the entire picture and plan each step carefully, you can almost guarantee your success. Should you truly want to succeed, you will find a way to do so. It's that simple. If you do what it takes to achieve it, you can get everything from life.

Keep in mind the old saying, "a *can't* never *could*". Think about that saying "How well do you really understand?" If you go through life thinking you can't do something, you never will. You both have to *think* that you can accomplish whatever you set your mind to, and more importantly, you have to *know* it.

Surround yourself with positive, happy people and avoid negative people, as they will only bring you down. When you begin telling others about your Internet dreams, you may hear, "Why on earth do you want to do that?" or "You must be crazy to think you can do that." Be an optimist. If you think about it, most negative people are those who are still working their nine to five jobs every day and probably always will. They never ventured out on their own and will never make any "REAL" money.

Remember... You'll NEVER make any real money working for someone else.

XXXX' Corporate Turnaround Centre

EXERCISE 4.1

ULTIMATE INTERNET MARKETING

Complete the following *Ultimate Internet Marketing Strategy* checklist

A True and Sincere Zeal	How passionate are you about your business, on a scale of 1 - 10?	
Your Personal Domain	Do you have your own domain name?	
Professional Website	How professional-looking is your website?	
Informative, Good Quality Content	What is the quality of your site content?	
Focused and Targeted Traffic	Are you getting enough traffic of the right type?	
Opt-in List (Ezine)	Do you have a publication (or similar) that enables you to have direct contact with your customer list?	
Your Own In-Demand Product	Is your product something that your customers want?	
Killer Sales Copy	How well does your sales pitch target the wants and needs of your customers?	
Killer Marketing Strategy	Review your strategy; is it up to date?	
Instantaneous Product Delivery	Can your customers place orders online and arrange delivery?	
Accept Credit Cards	Do you?	
Developing Credibility	What have you done lately to deserve your customers' trust?	
Presence	What offline presence do you have and how do you use it to drive traffic online?	

XXXX' Corporate Turnaround Centre

"Hail the Internet"

The Great Depression was a terrible time
Jobs and people fell into the grime
Now we're facing something similar
With financial uncertainty and profits irregular

But we have a new ace, up our sleeve
If we save our jobs then we don't have to grieve
I know you're thinking, "There's no safe bets"
But join with me and all hail the Internet.

Online auctions and click-dot strategy
Is the best way to shout "me me and me"
As it is hard to be number one
In a downturn, with nowhere to run

It is time to maximise marketing
To capture customers, and to do your thing
The world of marketing, you will never forget
If you join with me and all hail the Internet

Now is the time to get on the right track
Blogging and testimonials will keep you off the rack
There is no choice but to have a voice
Facebook and My Space is your chance to make noise

Let's not pretend this is going to be easy
Let's not pretend things will not be queasy
And you're right not to assume there are no safe bets
But you stand a fighting chance if you hail the Internet.

XXXX' Corporate Turnaround Centre

Productivity Measurements for Internet Marketing

Internet measurements use several terms that may not be familiar to all:

- IP Address: A number which identifies where an Internet computer is located; for this section the important feature is that two different homes likely have different IP addresses
- Visit: When a person navigates to a web-site, it is called a "visit"
- Visitor: Someone who visits a web-site
- Web-site versus web page: A business web-site usually includes multiple pages, such as "Home", "About", "Contact", and descriptions of products or services; a visitor views one page at a time
- Page-views: The number of times one page has been viewed (by a unique IP Address)
- Contact: An Internet visitor who makes contact by telephone, e-mail, on-line order or in-person. Software on the site can only track contacts that result from clicking within the page. Complete contact rates can only be determined if the organization regularly asks "Where did you learn about us"?

Internet productivity deals with ratios such as:

- Visitors per day (or any time period): the number of unique visitors to one or more pages of the web-site
- Page-views per day (or any time period)
- Contact Conversion rate: the number of contacts divided by the page views
- Sales Conversion rate: the number of sales divided by the page views

XXXX ' Corporate Turnaround Centre

- Change in page-views per day after an event, such as:
    - A press release or other mainstream media announcement
    - The start of a new mainstream advertising programme
    - An update to a web page
    - An announcement using social media

END OF MODULE #4

As part of the Resuscitation Phase, you have analysed the market, established your online presence and brand and your company now has its ultimate Internet marketing strategy. To continue the Resuscitation, move on to the next module which deals with improving quality, strengthening your brand identity and investing in future expansion.

~

XXXX ' Corporate Turnaround Centre

Additional Online Resources

The following books authored by Dr. Mike Teng are relevant to this module. Details are available by clicking on the website below for each book.

Internet Turnaround: The use of Internet marketing to turnaround companies

www.turnaroundinternet.com

"Internet Turnaround" is a step by step guide that will enable you to discover the rules of winning in the Internet business.

Link Baiting to improve your page ranking on search engines

www.linkbaitings.com

Link Baiting survives as the most productive marketing tool to Internet and SEO marketing. It has fully transformed this Internet marketing tool into a fully established form of attracting visitors and increasing rankings.

The ultimate Internet marketing strategies and tactics during turbulent times

www.ultimateinternetstrategy.com

This book gives an update on what is available in the Internet marketing arena - Search Engine Marketing, blogging, YouTube, Social Media, etc., and explains in simple language how to use them.

You can also visit Dr. Mike Teng's www.youtube.com/1103teng to watch the YouTube videos of some of the books.

Ultimate Internet marketing strategies and tactics

http://tinyurl.com/ultimateinternetstrategy

The Internet has taken over every business sector globally. Due to the current economic downturn, many companies are already closing down, or to save office rentals, employees are made to work from home. This will help the employees to cut down on travel and food expenses, as they can work conveniently without leaving their homes. This, in turn, will further lead to a greater exposure and usage of the Internet whereby they will indulge in home business, online purchasing and even online entertainment.

Time to teach new ways

http://tinyurl.com/timetoteachnewways

The Internet has opened up a whole New World of opportunity for even the smallest home-based business owner. There are countless numbers of new self-made millionaires that achieved their newfound success on the Internet. These new millionaires are no different from you and me. They built their Internet businesses from the ground up, found a niche and built their success one day at a time.

Hail the Internet

http://www.youtube.com/watch?v=7h1mWiZ8DNIhttp://tinyurl.com/hailtheinternet

Do you know what the biggest market in the world is? It is not Asia, U.S. or Europe, it is the Internet. The Internet is a powerful tool for small- or medium-size businesses to compete against the big boys in the industry. The Internet is an ideal platform for innovation, speed and flexibility - the strengths of small businesses. The offline or traditional media is dominated by big companies whereas the Internet is relatively untapped and low entry costs for small companies to compete against the big ones.

http://www.youtube.com/watch?v=yWHpsCH7ad0

Internet Marketing for a Successful Turnaround Strategy

http://tinyurl.com/internetturnaround

The online medium becomes an attractive option as people stay at home to cut down travelling costs, businesses give up office spaces, moving into homes to save rental costs, and home businesses increase as the unemployed operate businesses from homes. As people and businesses move to homes, the use of the Internet and other digital media increases for online entertainment, purchases and communication. This is also the segment that is not dominated by the big enterprises; the small- and medium-sized enterprises to some extent have some competitive advantages. The small- and medium-sized enterprises are more flexible and innovative, both of which attributes are necessary to operate successfully on the Internet. The other advantages of the use of the Internet to increase sales are that it offers a cheap alternative to marketing our products and services globally. It operates 24x7 and the entry costs to participating in this medium are low.

MODULE #5

PHASE TWO (Cont'd): BREAKING THE BOTTLENECK: RESUSCITATION Part II

A good resuscitation strategy is like a good booster shot, it can revive a dying business, minus the pains of surgery.

This module focuses on the remaining key steps of the resuscitation phase:

5. Using service quality
6. Strengthening your brand name
7. Investing in future expansion

USING SERVICE QUALITY

Nowadays, with a highly competitive business environment and rising customers' expectations, it is difficult for companies to stay in business by merely offering superior product features. As features become more homogeneous, customers are often in a quandary when making their purchase decisions based solely on those attributes. Some customers may then use pricing as a yardstick for their purchasing decisions. However, this may be an inaccurate guideline as there is a limit to price reductions that the company can make in order to gain market share. A more effective strategic formulation and implementation involves relying on other concepts such as uniqueness and difference in order to stand out in the very crowded marketplace.

Conversely, ineffective strategic formulation and implementation rely merely on concepts like imitation, being overly cautious, and blending in with the rest of the pack. A powerful and yet effective tool which can be used to differentiate one's product *vis-à-vis* the competitors' is service quality. Ultimately, whether a company sells hamburgers or real estate, the bottom-line depends on service quality. How the company handles the customers is often of more importance than the product *per se*. So often, a customer's perception of product quality is coloured by their gauge of the company's service quality. Surveys have shown that the majority of a company's customers would switch to alternative products or services if they were dissatisfied with the company's service. Therefore one competitive advantage that a company should endeavour to cultivate is an excellent service quality culture.

The more employees subscribe to its excellent service quality culture, the healthier the company. This is similar to culturing and growing good bacteria in the body. Our intestines have millions of bacteria, both good and bad. The bad ones have the potential to cause diseases, while good bacteria keep us healthy. A healthy population of good bacteria in our gut is important to ensure good health, to prevent the growth of bad bacteria, to maintain a healthy digestive system and to improve the immune system. In many countries including Singapore, the customer is treated like a king and is always right. The Japanese treat the customer as God or *akayakasuma wa kamisam desu*[8]. Japanese companies try to meet their customers' special needs (*anshin*[9]). This is because, culturally, Japanese customers expect prompt service and full support including the provision of spare parts. This concern for quality service originates from the Japanese concept of *giri*[10], which percolates into the Japanese culture to provide the best to their customers. The Japanese believe that the vendor's very existence is due to the customer. Hence, a successful vendor has to solve the customer's problem conscientiously. There is no compromise on service quality.

Successful companies "wow" their customers with innovative solutions, shoring up customers' loyalty and differentiating themselves from the rest of the pack. Through perpetually redefining and reinventing their business, such companies do not confine themselves to the products or services they are currently selling. Neither are they limited by any mission statement that restricts their business vision. Rather, their business is to apply their skills and resources

---

[8] *akayakasuma wa kamisam desu* : literally, *"the customer is God."*
[9] *anshin* : translated, *"peace of mind."*
[10] *giri* : meaning it is their *"obligation"* to provide quality service.

ingeniously towards solving their customers' problems and beyond. In the highly competitive new economy, the key to business success rests on how a company unlocks these to address its customers' unique idiosyncrasy.

Such are the fundamental ways a company can distinguish and edge itself above the competition and forge relationships with customers, and thereby engender their loyalty and genuinely transform its products or services into value-added ones.

STRENGTHENING YOUR BRAND NAME

In the long term, the ailing organisation needs to build a strong brand name, as this will help resuscitate its business. A brand is the proprietary visual, emotional, rational and cultural image that you associate with a company or a product. The American Marketing Association defines a brand as a name, term, sign, symbol or design, or a combination of them, intended to identify the goods or services of one seller or group of sellers, and to differentiate them from those of competitors.

Marketing is the battling of the mindset to get your brand into your customer's mind. Customers can only remember a limited number of brands in their minds. Jack Trout said, *"One brand, one idea."* Brands help the customers to remember the products. Thus, when you think of Mercedes, it suggests luxury, success, prestige, fast speed, well-engineered, customer service *par excellence* and good resale value. When you think of Volvo, you might think of safety, thanks to the solid-as-a-tank bodywork. When you think of Nike, you might think of Michael Jordan or "Just Do It". When you think of Coffee, you might recall Starbucks. When you think of hamburgers, you might recall McDonald's. This is why a former chairman of Quaker Oats said: "If this business were to be split up, I would be glad to take the brands, trademarks and goodwill, and you could have all the bricks and mortar – and I would fare better than you." Even Bill Gates conceded that the success of Windows is not in the technology per se but rather the marketing of the brand. If you analyse success, it has a lot to do with the marketing of brand names.

Scott Bedbury, the man who gave the world 'Just Do It' and popularized 'Frappuccino' once said "A great brand is hard to find. I walked through a hardware store last night and I came across 50 brands I didn't know existed. They may be great products, but they're not great brands." Scott Bedbury later went on to be senior vice president of marketing at Starbucks Coffee Co and was responsible for growing the $700 million Seattle-based company into a global brand. In one of his brand-building principles Bedbury said, "To keep a brand alive over the long haul, to keep it vital, you've got to do something new, something unexpected. It has to be related to the brand's core position. But every once in a while you have to strike out in a new direction, surprise the consumer, add a new dimension to the brand, and reenergize it."

A powerful brand is said to have high brand equity. Brand equity is the added value endowed upon a product or service as a result of past investments in the marketing of the brand. The higher the brand equity, the higher the brand loyalty, name awareness, perceived quality, strong brand associations and other assets such as patents, trademarks and channel relationships. As an asset, a brand name needs to be carefully managed so that its brand equity does not depreciate. This requires constant maintenance and improvement of the brand awareness, brand perceived quality and functionality, positive brand associations, and so on over time. It also requires continuous R&D investment, skilful advertising promotion and re-creation. Unfortunately, companies do not normally list brand equity on their balance sheets because of the somewhat arbitrary nature of its estimate.

INVESTING IN FUTURE EXPANSIONS

Once most of the basic resuscitation measures are in place, the turnaround CEO can focus on investing for future expansions. Subject to availability of resources, these could take the form of expansion in production facilities, business ventures (individually or on a joint basis) and even mergers and acquisitions (M&As), both locally and overseas. Capital injections are required for most of these expansion strategies. If the company's resources are limited, it could expand through sharing of facilities, joint-product development or marketing, joint-venture or consortium participations for large projects, etc. The latter strategy is particularly effective when expanding overseas for companies with constraints in funds and resources and wishing to limit the risks.

Some M&As are necessary to enable companies to remain competitive in their industries. With business going global at a seemingly ferocious pace, companies are compelled to join forces through M&A just to keep up. Some companies that today are household names, such as General Motors and General Electric, were formed through a series of acquisitions years ago. Successful M&As are hard to come by, but it is necessary in some industries. For instance, as major corporations they spread their tentacles worldwide, they do not like dealing with hundreds of little telecommunication suppliers. Mergers between these telecommunication companies to build global capability probably make sense. In the case of the banking industry, M&A is used to extend market reach. Some logistics companies have explained going to M&A to increase capacity, to amortise the heavy investment in computer systems and operations management across as broad a base as possible. Many companies merge to increase shareholder value, because some stock markets simply love a merger.

XXXX ' Corporate Turnaround Centre

Many well-managed companies are able to enhance shareholder value with rare, small, prudent acquisitions that fit neatly into their larger strategic plan. And although this plan is aimed at addressing the challenges of tomorrow's marketplace, many M&As do not work out or produce the results expected by the acquiring companies. The fact is, a vicious cycle of acquisitions–divestitures seems to prevail. Today's acquisition for "synergy" soon becomes tomorrow's divestiture in order to "get back to core businesses", which is then paradoxically followed by tomorrow's merger for "operational efficiency", which in turn is followed by tomorrow's breakup to "get back to basics", and it goes on and on. In planning M&As, the turnaround CEO must be mindful of certain pitfalls.

Pitfall Number 1: No Homework Done

This is one of the common pitfalls of many companies seeking to embark upon expansion. Expansions are often done hastily and without proper evaluation, or support from adequate market research and survey. Decisions are often made in order to accomplish business expansion as part of its corporate objectives and the risk factors are ignored. One common mistake is to apply the "China statistics" when the sums are being done. The assumption is that with 1.3 billion people in China, if we are able to obtain one percent of the market share, this translates into 1.3 million of captured customers. What an impressive market by any measuring yardstick! Urged on by such simple statistics, many foreign investors invested heavily and aggressively in China. Unfortunately, to their dismay, they soon learned that China is still a third world country. The bulk of the population is too poor to pay for some of their products and services. The immutable law in marketing applies, that is "You cannot make money from people who do not have money." Also, some of these expansions may not tie in coherently with the company's long-term plans.

XXXX · Corporate Turnaround Centre

Many sick SMEs are deluded by the notion that overseas expansions will help solve their financial woes, as pastures seem greener elsewhere. However, it is better for them to fix their domestic problems first, as expanding overseas would further stretch their limited resources. Also, operating overseas may pose other hazards which may not be anticipated. Sadly, there are also many multinationals which embarked upon major M&As but failed miserably. Sometimes, proper homework as well as rational thinking will reveal that it is better to buy the key people and grow the business rather than buy the company. It may be a cheaper and easier alternative.

A more recent example is that of the September 15, 2008 merger between Bank of America and Merrill Lynch. This merger was surrounded by complications ranging from employee bonuses, added debt and forced hands as evident in the April 13, 2009 U.S. Senate Committee on Banking investigation of the merger. But the merger in which Bank of America agreed to pay about $50 billion in stock for Merrill soured at light speed. Back then, the combined companies, which would have been valued by the stock market at about $176 billion, fell to around $40 billion in 2009.

Pitfall Number 2: Wrong Timing

The success of expansion also hinges largely on the right timing. An old Chinese saying states that for a business to flourish, you need to have the correct timing. If a company ventures into a particular market too early in the product life cycle (that is, at the introduction stage), it may not be able to reap the full benefits of such expansion, as the ground may be hard and it has to invest substantial resources into developing the market. In the process, the early participants may end up paying high "tuition" fees as they learn from their mistakes.

XXXX ' Corporate Turnaround Centre

If a company enters the market too late (that is, at the saturation or decline stage), it runs the risk of curtailing its future growth potential, as competition will be very intense. Examples include the proliferation of many dot.com companies and telecom start-ups just prior to the bursting of the high-tech stocks bubble.

The best time to enter a market is during the growth stage. The ability to recognise this opportunity is critical. Both IBM and Digital Equipment Corporation (DEC) had better access to the technology than Bill Gates and Paul Allen, but these giants limit the scope of their technology to serving their existing corporate customers with their existing and constantly upgraded products. Consequently, both companies missed the PC's precursors – the dedicated electronic word processors that made Wang Computers successful. The latter, in turn, did not see - as Microsoft did - that personal computers could replace word processors by executing far more functions than word-processing. Therefore, no one at IBM, DEC or Wang Computers took much notice of the MITS Altair 8800: the "World's First Microcomputer Kit to Rival Commercial Models." That headline in *Popular Electronics* magazine in January 1974 inspired Gates and Allen to write a version of the well-known BASIC computer knowledge for the machine to run on. The rest is history. In the book, *The Road Ahead*[33], Bill Gates remarked: "Getting in on the first stages of the PC revolution looked like the opportunity of a lifetime, and we seized it."

Pitfall Number 3: Ego Trap

Success can bring forth the ego trap if we are not careful. Many big companies let success go to their head. According to Peter Littmann, CEO of Hugo Boss, these successful companies started to think they know the right answers, which is never true because there *are* no right answers. If you deal with contemporary art, it will teach you very fast that there are many answers and some of them are right and wrong at the same time. Thus, when the euphoria soars, the CEO must exercise more care and not fall into the "ego" trap. This can cause him to be over zealous in accomplishing the corporate expansion objectives and impair his sense of perspective. This is why somebody said, "Egotism is the quality that causes a person to think he's in the groove when he's actually in a rut."

A classic example is Carly Fiorina. In July 1999, Hewlett-Packard named Fiorina chief executive officer succeeding Lewis Platt and prevailing over the internal candidate Ann Livermore. She became the first woman to lead a Fortune 20 company. Fiorina proceeded to break up HP and merged the part she kept with the PC maker Compaq. Although the decision to spin-off the company's technical equipment division predated her arrival, one of her first major responsibilities as chief executive was overseeing the successful separation of the unit into the standalone Agilent Technologies. In 2002, in the wake of the bursting of the Tech Bubble, Fiorina spearheaded a controversial merger with Compaq, a leading competitor in the industry. Fiorina fought for the merger, and it was implemented despite strong opposition from board member Walter Hewlett (the son of company co-founder William Hewlett) who claimed that the merger was being pursued by Fiorina in desperation to make a strategic decision and to give her some breathing space from Wall Street.

In early January 2005, the Hewlett-Packard board of directors discussed with Fiorina a list of issues that the board had regarding the company's performance. The board proposed a plan to shift her authority to HP division heads, which Fiorina resisted. Less than a month later, the board brought back in Tom Perkins and forced Fiorina to resign as chairman and chief executive officer of the company. The company's stock jumped on news of Fiorina's departure. Under the company's agreement with Fiorina, she was paid slightly more than twenty million dollars in severance. When Fiorina became CEO in July, 1999, HP's stock price was $52 per share, and when she left 5 1/2 years later in February, 2005, it was $21 per share—a loss of over 60% of the stock's value. During this same time period, HP competitor Dell's stock price increased from $37 to $40 per share.

Pitfall Number 4: Preference for Buying Success Rather Than Earning It

Increasingly, there is preference for short-cutting the corporate success formula through acquisition rather than organic growth. While some acquisition activities constitute prudent strategy, management which relies solely on portfolio strategies to enhance market share and earnings growth are more likely to drive their companies' profits and stock values down.

Management must keep in perspective the company's long-term vision and sense of coherent purpose. Otherwise the M&As may be misconstrued as the magical elixir for its salvation.

Pitfall Number 5: Rapid Expansion Can Be Fatal

While fast growth is a most exciting phase for running a business, it is also a much more risky time than assumed. Rapid expansion done in haste with inadequate homework, wrong timing, egoistic reasons and impatience for success can result in calamity. However, if investments in expansions are decided upon and implemented correctly, they can resuscitate the company. Financial due diligence of the business is necessary for an independent assessment of the business and its financial information. Hire accountants to do this job for you. Meet with the accountants before drawing up the terms of reference in order to establish a realistic 24-hour time frame and to agree on the costs. You should liaise between your accountants doing the financial due diligence and your lawyers who are looking into the other aspects of due diligence. This will ensure that you do not waste time and money in duplicating the due diligence, and that all areas are covered within the time frame. The main objective of the financial due diligence is to obtain specific financial, commercial and administrative information regarding the business including but not limited to the following:

- constitution and structure of the business
- capital structure of the business
- shareholding pattern
- shareholder rights
- current position of assets and liabilities of the business
- summary of latest net asset position
- review of financial position, including financing arrangements
- working capital requirements, contingent liabilities
- summary of the last three years' profit and loss account
- accounting policies
- tax affairs of the business

Nowadays, environmental due diligence has become an essential component of due diligence. There are a number of reasons why environmental liabilities are relevant to your purchase:

- The control over certain business activities that can affect the environment are increasing by the day and becoming more complex
- Insurance against environmental liabilities is difficult to obtain.
- Public opinion
- Under the existing laws, liability for violation of an environmental law will fall on the original polluter who has knowingly permitted the polluting material to remain in the land. However, if such persons cannot be found, the present owner or occupier may become liable to carry out remedial measures that can be very expensive and thus affect the bottom line of the business.

Environmental due diligence is necessary to determine the extent and the nature of risk involved in buying a business and becoming responsible for its liabilities. You must make sure that the business complies with all the environmental regulations and has all 25 necessary permits and clearance from the relevant authorities for carrying on the business. Your accountants must investigate the tax position of the business. Verifying the accuracy of the information is essential. The main purpose of a tax due diligence is to determine the existence of any potential exposure to a tax liability.

Another purpose of tax due diligence is to ensure that the valuation of the business can be properly ascertained. Tax due diligence will establish whether the business' tax affairs are currently in order and whether there could be any sudden tax liabilities that could arise in the near future. Use the tax due diligence to identify the tax-saving opportunities that you can take advantage of after you buy the business. The extent of due diligence you conduct is based on many factors, including the size of the transaction, the likelihood of closing a transaction, tolerance for risk, time constraints, cost factors, and resource availability. It is impossible to learn everything about a business but it is important to learn enough such that you lower your risks to acceptable levels and make good, informed business decisions.

Time allocated for due diligence can vary widely with each situation. Time schedules through the closing of a business purchase transaction are typically tight. You should ensure that adequate time is allocated to due diligence. Maintain confidentiality of all information that you have access to during due diligence. When you are conducting due diligence, it is also necessary that you have the most important resource necessary to own the business – finance. All your efforts of dealing with the seller and conducting the due diligence will be a waste of time and money if you haven't lined up your finances. You won't get far in your endeavour of buying and owning a business without it.

Assuming you have the requisite financial backing and have performed your due diligence, what else remains? You might start by reviewing the plans for productivity and innovation improvements...just a few pages ahead. Then, once you have ensured that your company will stay alive, the next task will be to begin long-term therapy to make it healthy and competitive.

EXERCISE 5.1
RESUSCITATING YOUR COMPANY, PART II

To focus your attention on resuscitation and the contents of this module, consider the following questions in relation to your company.

5. **To what degree do you focus on service quality? How do you know what your customers think of your service?**

6. **How strong is your brand name? What is your brand equity worth? How can you improve that?**

7. **What expansion pitfalls have you fallen into in the past? What pitfalls are in front of you now?**

XXXX' Corporate Turnaround Centre

Productivity Measurements for Phase 2 Part 2

Sample productivity measurements in this phase include:

- Responding to customer complaints to your call centre:
  - Average number of calls per customer per complaint before the issue is resolved
  - Average time spent "on the phone" to resolve one complaint
  - Average time elapsed to resolve one complaint so the customer is back in service
  - Average number of people required to handle one customer's complaint (including the first contact, supervisors, schedulers and dispatchers, spare-parts inventory and logistics clerks, and technical service personnel)

This is the time to re-sample the "**Productivity Measurements for Phase 2 Part 1**", which followed **Exercise 3.1**. Has your company improved since then?

Innovation Culture Measurements for Phase 2 Part 2

High performance, consistent innovation, productivity and so many more qualities of successful organizations are not the results of "just luck". A successful and mature company has established systematic processes to ensure the best outcomes in each endeavour. The questions in this section help to identify where your organization is well-prepared or where it needs to improve.

Only by pursuing the twin goals of productivity and innovation can a company gain and retain a competitive edge. New and innovative methods for improving productivity are required, since other organizations also seek ways to cut costs and produce more with less. Applying systematic productivity tools to the task of creating innovations will be required, since other competitors are busy inventing new products which may render yours obsolete.

Several of the criteria that are required for a successful Innovation Culture are:

- Quality: the Six Sigma discipline may be the most famous innovator for improving quality
- Problem Finders: people who notice bottlenecks and set out to make improvements
- Resources for Innovators: the organization must provide resources to support innovation
- Organizational Infrastructure must support the goals established by the company
- Rules and regulations: innovative companies strike a balance between flexibility and enforcement
- Leadership: does the management team pro-actively seek and develop new opportunities?

XXXX ' Corporate Turnaround Centre

- Creativity must be nourished in an innovative organization
- Failure: does the company punish a failed attempt at innovation, or does it learn?
- Performance of Individuals: are employees rewarded for their achievements?
- Individual Contributions must be recognized and appreciated
- Does the organization support the employees in Skills Development?
- External Environment: a company in survival mode will innovate for survival; one that is flourishing must innovate to continue succeeding in the future
- Response to individual problems: does the company help an employee or leave him floundering?

The **Innovation Culture in Ninety Questions** ™ tool uses a set of ninety questions to evaluate a company on these key factors.

END OF MODULE #5

Boosting the quality of the service throughout your company's operation and strengthening your brand, you are now looking to future expansion – quite possibly a big difference from where you started in module #1! Resuscitation is over, now is the time for Therapy and the next module.

~

XXXX' Corporate Turnaround Centre

Additional Online Resources

The following books authored by Dr. Mike Teng are relevant to modules #3 and #5, covering the Resuscitation Phase. Details are available by clicking on the website below for each book.

Fundamentals of Buying and Selling of Companies
www.restructuringspecialist.com
This book is written in a simple and easy-to-understand manner on the complex topic of mergers and acquisitions and what to do look for when buying and selling companies.

Buying and selling of distressed companies
www.restructuringexpert.com
Investing in distressed assets can prove to be very profitable, as they are at rock bottom prices. This book dwells into the nitty-gritty of what to do look for when identifying such gems.

You can also visit Dr. Mike Teng's www.youtube.com/1103teng **to watch the YouTube videos of some of the book.**

Beware of the merger
http://tinyurl.com/bewareofmerger
Merger is a good corporate turnaround and transformation strategy. However, the majority of mergers do not add value to the shareholders. This is because companies merge for all the wrong reasons and with no homework done, basically ego reasons. CEOs find it quicker and more glamorous to grow by merging rather than organic growth. They fail to integrate the stakeholders and the organizations properly and thus, the result is failure.

Going for public listing

http://tinyurl.com/publiclisting

Many SMEs want to go for public listing so that the founders can make their money and retire. However, these founders need to make sure that their companies are ready. The corporate governance and compliance are getting very tight and strict in many jurisdictions. There are advantages with public listing, such as making the profile of the firm more visible. Outsiders feel more comfortable dealing with a listed company as its financial reporting is more transparent. Insiders also feel proud working for a listed firm.

Buying a company

http://tinyurl.com/buyingacompany

Everyone wants to be his or her own boss. The easiest way to do this is to have your own business. You can own a business and be your own boss, but to own a business, you either need to start your own business or buy an existing one. Starting a business is not for everyone but yes, just about anyone and everyone can buy an existing business.

Buying distressed companies

http://tinyurl.com/distressedassets

Distressed securities include stocks, bonds or other financial claims of a company that is close to or has reached financial distress. If a company has filed for bankruptcy, it is under financial distress. This category also includes bank debt and non-performing loans. They fail to make regular interest or principal payments, and they trade at yields higher than those of similar dated treasuries. Once their financial distress becomes evident, there is panic selling and they then trade at deep discounts. At this stage, they present an attractive opportunity to anyone who has analyzed their true worth. In recent years, private firms such as hedge funds and private equity firms have been among the largest buyers of distressed securities. They hold the securities until they have appreciated, and then sell them.

MODULE #6

PHASE THREE:

THERAPY Part I

"Turbulent times need inspired leaders"

It is easy to rule and make important decisions
When the profits are good and do not need incisions
It is easy to rule when good times are rocking
And criticisms of your style are not knocking

The times, though, have turned; they are no longer good
The times have got rough, and profits are not as they should
The time for change management has arrived
The time for change management is not contrived

Chorus
Turbulent times call for leaders and inspiring people
Turbulent times are being shouted from the steeples
The world has changed and we must all stand as one
And leaders become heroes, and do what must be done

Some people are born to lead, others to follow
But we all have a role and all want to wallow
In good times and a good world of prosperity
Which is peaceful and for all to love and see

Leaders such as President Obama are having a hard time
Leaders such as Bernake have to relearn their lines
For they recognise the need for change management
They recognise the old ways are just entanglement

Chorus
Turbulent times call for leaders and inspiring people
Turbulent times are being shouted from the steeples
The world has changed and we must all stand as one
And leaders become heroes, and do what must be done

Thinking and planning is the only way to succeed
In addressing the problems, addressing world need
If we look at things differently then we have the idea
If we look at things studiously, then answers are clear

Leaders everywhere face an economic crisis
Leaders everywhere face much economic unrest
But the good ones know the answers are in demand
The clever ones have them now, and are saving the land

Chorus
Turbulent times call for leaders and inspiring people
Turbulent times are being shouted from the steeples
The world has changed and we must all stand as one
And leaders become heroes, and do what must be done

WHAT IS THE THERAPY PHASE?

The essence of the Therapy phase hinges upon the building of a strong and healthy corporate culture by incorporating a new corporate philosophy and strengthening the free flow of internal energy. It is equivalent to having a strong "corporate immune system" with an action-driven orientation, namely flexible, fast and focused so that the organisation can combat the mutating and aggressive viruses.

Central in this phase is the interplay between the concepts of a new and dynamic corporate philosophy and *qi*, or internal energy, as symbolised by the dualistic concept of *yin* and *yang*. The Chinese characters for *yin* and *yang* mean literally the shady side and sunny side, respectively. *Yin* symbolises the feminine qualities of the universe while *yang* signifies the masculine qualities.

The *qi*, which is more oriented towards the oriental philosophy (more indirect), acts on the *yin* of the body. On the other hand, the corporate philosophy which is more oriented towards the Western concept (more direct) acts on the *yang* element. They are different dimensions of the fundamental corporate tenets essential for engendering a strong and healthy corporate culture and fostering resilience within the organisation. All these form the core beliefs – the foundation of corporate culture vital for successful corporate rehabilitation or renewal. These core beliefs tell people what is sacred, what is sanctioned and what is taboo.

A company should strive to create a new and dynamic corporate philosophy that encapsulates basic beliefs and values such as the generation of new ideas, acceptance of changes and willingness to accept failure. Coexisting with its corporate philosophy in the company is the *qi* or internal energy which is the drive and passion. The free flow of internal energy and its interaction with the prevalent corporate philosophy in turn create powerful catalytic and synergistic effects within the organisation. Supporting these core beliefs of the corporate philosophy and *qi* are the other pre-requisites or qualities that act like therapies in fostering the instillation of a strong and healthy corporate culture.

These are quite similar to those non-drug-based therapies for strengthening one's physical immune system, such as having a positive mental attitude, active communication, as well as eating and exercising well. All these function together like spokes, linking the inner core belief to the wheel of the management mantra of the organisation, enmeshing the desired characteristics of the company's action-driven orientation: being fast, flexible and focused. The smooth operation of both the inner and outer circles will provide the company with clock-work precision enabling it to operate trouble-free as well as fortifying it against the ravages of viral attacks and other perils that may threaten its existence.

Therefore, the Therapy phase is a longevity booster that can be used to extend the upper limit of a corporation's life span. It is also noted earlier that even the best surgical and resuscitation strategies may be doomed or encounter difficulties in their implementation if the staff involved do not back up the turnaround CEO or wholeheartedly believe in those strategies. This inability to solicit full commitment is often closely linked to the company's corporate culture and "heart" issues. Hence, a company without the right corporate culture and "heart" issues will fail in the long term even if its surgery or resuscitation strategies (Phases I and II) are in order. For centuries, we have been told of the importance of the heart. As the adages go: "Listen to your heart", "As a man thinks in his heart so is he" and "Let your heart be right, it does not matter where the head lies." A person can be brain dead with his heart still functioning. However, once the heart stops beating, the brain will be dead very quickly. Similarly, the brain helps to analyse and strategize, but it is the heart that fosters the understanding and commitment so critical for corporate success. Thus, a Therapy phase is necessary to address the "heart" issues for holistic recovery.

We also address office politics half-way through Phase III, because we are social beings. Success or failure in business is based largely on relationships: co-operative or competitive; honest or underhanded; friendly or antagonistic. Each of us must work for individual success and also for the good of the organization that pays the salary and performance bonus.

INCORPORATING A NEW CORPORATE PHILOSOPHY

The corporate philosophy is a unique set of thoughts and values of an organisation. It communicates how people in the organisation should behave by establishing a value system and by conveying that value system through its actions. The wrong philosophy will set in motion the wrong thought processes and this, in turn, will trigger the wrong manifestation of behavioural patterns and values, which are basically the corporate culture.

The turnaround CEO's primary task here is to reorient the entire company's corporate philosophy or mindset along the following fundamental tenets:
- New ideas and ways of doing things
- Acceptance of change as a constant
- Willingness to accept failure as a result

This new corporate philosophy sounds like motherhood statements. It normally constitutes the bedrock or pillar of the company's declared value and thought system at its inception. However, with the passage of time, the values or basic tenets of the company's corporate philosophy may become diluted or taken for granted, thereby losing its efficacy. Just like a drug loses its efficacy after being put on the shelf for too long, some of these timeless philosophical concepts get forgotten. Therefore, it is important for the company to periodically remind itself of this cornerstone corporate philosophy to ensure that there is no substantial deviation or omission along its corporate journey. This does not imply that the other noble aspects and values of corporate philosophy, such as responsibilities to society and environment, ethical code of conduct and respect for the individual are unimportant. However, the core or fundamental tenets have been singled out and espoused here as their applications have a decisive impact on the degree of success in the company's rehabilitation efforts.

XXXX ' Corporate Turnaround Centre

New Ideas and Ways of Doing Things

Central in the new corporate philosophy is the belief that in the new knowledge economy, ideas are the raw materials that the company can utilise or tap into in order to leapfrog ahead of competition and to create new opportunities or avenues for its growth. Basically, there is no such concept as a "bad idea". Winners must be like immigrants – able to see new ideas and determined to succeed.

One such example is Twitter, a social networking and microblogging service that enables its users to send and read messages known as tweets. Since its creation in 2006 by Jack Dorsey, Twitter has gained notability and popularity worldwide. It is sometimes described as "SMS[11] of the Internet." The use of Twitter's application programming interface for sending and receiving text messages by other applications often eclipses direct use of Twitter. Twitter began in a "daylong brainstorming session" that was held by board members of the podcasting company Odeo in an attempt to break a creative slump. During that meeting, Jack Dorsey introduced the idea of an individual using an SMS service to communicate with a small group, a concept partially inspired by the SMS group messaging service.

On March 2010, Twitter has recorded a 1,500 percent growth in the number of registered users. The number of its employees has grown 500 percent, while over 70,000 registered apps have been created for this microblogging platform, according to the first email newsletter on the company's progress by the website's co-founder Biz Stone. By the end of 2007, about 500,000 tweets per quarter were posted. By the end of 2008, 100 million tweets per quarter were posted. By the end of 2009, 2 billion tweets per quarter were posted. In the first quarter of 2010, 4 billion tweets per quarter were posted. The revenue

---

[11] SMS: literally, *"Short Message Service"* – the text communication service component that allows the exchange of short text messages between fixed line or mobile phone devices.

projections for the end of 2013 were $1.54 billion in revenue, $111 million in net earnings, and 1 billion users.

Acceptance of Change as a Constant

Organisations that can outwit and outlast competitors are those who are continually staying nimble, springy and forward-looking by living and breathing change. Turnaround CEOs endeavouring to revive their companies must invest considerable efforts to re-educate the staff that change is a permanent feature in corporate life. Basking in past glories and maintaining the *status quo* will only generate complacency. Hence, the staff has to constantly re-evaluate and refocus their goals and roles. This will enable them to meet the myriad of challenges confronting the new corporate landscape.

It is only when this part of the corporate philosophy has fully permeated from the top management to the lowest rank staff that the company is able to acquire the fluidity to adapt and re-invent itself quickly. This is an increasingly turbulent world in which most of the products and services are rapidly becoming obsolete. Hence, the antidote for managing the future lies not in administering the placebo of lip service, piecemeal fire-fighting measures or reactive strategies, but in having the next product ready when the market opportunity arises. This also means drastic reduction in time lags and being always ready for any exigencies. All these demand radical changes in the attitudes and reactions of management. They should perceive that changes are not threats but opportunities that are inexhaustible in changing markets or markets engineered to change – all these can create and reap success. To thrive, you need to destroy, create and rebuild with this process repeated several times if necessary.

Willingness to Accept Failure as a Result

The famous inventor, Thomas Edison, is a classic illustration of the need to accept change and the willingness to accept failure. He performed several thousand experiments before finally discovering the right filament to be used in the light bulb. He was ridiculed by a university professor who said: "Thomas, don't be a fool. Light does not come from wire, it comes from fire." Fire was the norm of providing light in those days. Nevertheless, Edison was not discouraged by this remark and continued relentlessly with his experiments using wires. He found the right filament a few months after this incident.

Many of life's failures are people who did not realise how close they were to success at the point when they gave up. When he was interviewed by a reporter on his success, he was asked: "Sir, how did you persevere after a few thousand times of failure?" Edison's reply was that it was not a few thousand times of failure but rather a few thousand steps to the right solution.

FREE-FLOWING INTERNAL ENERGY

What is Internal Energy (Qi)?

One concept that is central to Chinese medicine but which the Western scientific world is still struggling to accept is an internal substance that the Chinese call *qi* (internal energy). In the West, it is sometimes described as part bio-chemical and part electromagnetic energy. You cannot examine it under a microscope; nor can you detect it with scientific instruments. This is not to say that one cannot feel it or see it, but these are intuitive human qualities that practitioners of Chinese medicine develop over years of practice. It is everyone's birthright to have *qi*. You can perceive this *qi* energy in a more subtle manner. Martial arts experts practising *gongfu* (or *Kung Fu*) sometimes feel it as heat in the palms of their hands that can extinguish a candle flame without touching it with their palms. It is a warmth in the body that enables *gongfu* proponents' bodies to be hit by hard objects without sustaining injuries. It is used to describe air, breath of life or vital essence by proponents of *Qigong* and *Taiji*. A person's health is closely linked to his level of *qi*.

Qi in Chinese Medicine

Qi issues are paramount in treating chronic problems and strengthening the immune system, thereby initiating healing and preventive qualities. Ill-health is often associated with the blockage of one's *qi*. If one is ill, such clearance will result in the normalisation and re-establishment of optimal functioning of one's body and most diseases should disappear. If one is not ill, the free flow of *qi* will further enhance the existing sense of wellness and well-being. According to the Chinese medical theory, many diseases arise from adverse environmental conditions such as heat, cold, wind, dryness and humidity; wrong diet; spoiled food; worms and microbes; poisoning and pollution; trauma and accidents. In our analogy, these are external viruses affecting companies. Internal conditions can arise from excess or deficient emotions of anger, joy, sympathy, grief or fear and inappropriate mental attitudes and beliefs (such as anxiety and stress). These are also maladies of the spirit which can cause serious problems. In Module #1 we identified these as internally-generated viruses that attack companies. All the above factors can cause one's *qi* to become excessive, deficient, stuck, blocked, congested or stagnant, resulting in all sorts of problems. When the immune system is strong, one is emotionally centred within one's body and the *qi* and blood are flowing freely, then most diseases should disappear.

The goal of ancient Oriental healings such as *tui na*[12], acupuncture and the practising of *qigong, taiji, gongfu*, are to enable the *qi* to circulate strongly and

---

[12] Chinese therapies to treat injuries, pains using massage, Chinese herbal bandages, etc.

unobstructed within the body to strengthen the immune system. This helps the person to resist or overcome imbalances or blockages resulting in disharmonies. Once the human body is able to regain its state of dynamic equilibrium, it is able to generate its own healing.

Qi in the Western Context

In the corporate Western context, *qi* is the human spirit, drive, passion and energy. It is the same *qi* that keeps you awake when you are watching the World Cup matches or your favourite television program. *Qi* is the relentless drive for progress: a drive that arises from the deep human urge to explore, create and improve.

Similar to the corporate philosophy, the drive for progress (*qi*) is an internal force. It does not wait for the external world to say it is time to change, time to improve or time to invent something new. Like the drive of a great artist, inventor or prolific investor, it is simply there, impelling and propelling ahead.

Through a drive for progress, or *qi*, the company displays a powerful mix of self-confidence and self-criticism. The self-confidence element allows the company to make audacious goals, bold and daring moves, sometimes even risking and defying conventional wisdom or strategic prudence. On the other hand, self-criticism pushes for self-induced change and improvements before the outside world imposes the need to do so. In Phase III, the company should be its harshest critic.

Qi and the New Corporate Philosophy

As seen earlier, the interplay between the corporate philosophy and *qi* or internal energy is crucial. Both these elements co-exist much like the *yin* and *yang* of the Chinese dualistic philosophy. Each element of this *yin* and *yang* concept is dependent on the other, complementing and reinforcing each other, creating synergistic benefits. The company should not just seek mere balance between the corporate philosophy and *qi*. It should attempt to be both highly ideological in its corporate philosophy, yet highly progressive in *qi* simultaneously. For instance, Sun Tzu also mentioned the use of this *qi* energy in his military philosophy when he said: "The clever combatant looks to the effect of combined energy, and does not require too much from individuals.

XXXX ' Corporate Turnaround Centre

Hence his ability to pick out the right men and utilise combined energy. When he utilises the combined energy, his fighting men became as it were like unto rolling logs or stones... Thus the energy developed by good fighting men is as the momentum of a round stone rolled down a mountain thousands of feet in height."

The best way to build a strong corporate immune system is to allow free flow of the human energy. This is preventive medicine, for a strong immune system can prolong the life, and enhance the vitality and well-being of the person. Similarly, a corporate culture with the philosophy that allows free flow of the human energy and spirit can help ward off internal and external viruses. A successful organisation is one that is able to unleash the powers of its people to exploit change, even in the midst of crisis or in the face of an obstacle. Therefore the key strategic questions for the CEO and each member of his management team are:

- What is your current *qi* level?
- What should your future *qi* level be?
- What impact will your *qi* level have on the future outlook of your products, markets and customers?

Understanding the concept of *qi* is fundamental to the success of a business. *Qi* is the predominant component of any business. In addition to assessing the staff's IQ (intelligence quotient) and EQ (emotional quotient), companies should assess the staff's *QiQ* (internal energy quotient). It will allow the company to formulate a strategy that will equip it with a distinctive and sustainable advantage, thereby enabling it to leapfrog ahead and render competition almost irrelevant.

XXXX' Corporate Turnaround Centre

A STRONG AND HEALTHY CORPORATE CULTURE

Corporate culture is collectively an internalised deeply embedded set of beliefs, expectations and assumptions that influences and guides the thinking and behaviour among organisation members. It is extremely important, as its pervasive influence can literally destroy or promote a corporation's ability to compete and succeed. It is distinct and exists in every organisation.

Going back to the medical analogy, a strong and healthy corporate culture is like a strong immune system, helping the company to combat viruses. It embraces the concept of the new corporate philosophy and *qi*, and engenders action orientation by being flexible, fast and focused. When a person falls sick, he usually takes medication to heal his condition. However, some of these medications or drugs may cause side-effects. Sometimes, the best medication is no medication at all. Do not think of drugs as cures, think of them as poisons. Likewise, in the case of a company, the best form of defence against viral attacks is to build up and strengthen its corporate culture or immune system. A weak immune system can kill a person.

A troubled company too has a corporate culture, albeit a dysfunctional one. Many studies have found that excellent corporations have a strong corporate culture that is based on the right philosophy and is marked by a culturally-driven set of priorities that recapture the drive, passion and internal energy of the people. All these provide the employees with a sense of direction, belonging and destiny. Once the desired new corporate philosophy and internal energy are in place, there will be a natural progression towards instillation of a strong and healthy corporate culture. An important factor that determines whether this strong and healthy corporate culture is achievable in a company is its employees.

XXXX ' Corporate Turnaround Centre

What Types of Employees and Leaders are Required?

The next question is: What types of employees and leaders are required in this new corporate culture? Just as there is "good" and "bad" for our bodies, similarly, in every organisation, there are two categories of employees. There are the "outside-in" or "bad" cholesterol employees as well as the "inside-out" or "good" cholesterol employees. Those in the first category, the "bad" cholesterol, are not natural self-starters and they require prodding by some external forces from the environment before they are compelled towards achieving certain set goals. Too much of the "bad" cholesterol can increase risk of heart attack and stroke, as the "bad" cholesterol slowly builds up in the walls of the arteries that feed the heart and brain.

The leadership during Phase III also needs to take on a softer approach unlike the earlier phases. During this phase, the turnaround CEO needs to empower more. Organisations need to fire up their employees' commitment and passion. The spiritual leader has the means to ignite that internal energy. Only the spiritual leader – one who is able to initiate and unleash the internal energy of the employees – can lead a future successful organisation. The spiritual leader can relieve and purge all the constipated negative thoughts of the employees - the equivalent of toxins - from the organisation. The spiritual leader does this by inspiring others. Those of us who lead - whether we have a title or not - need to view ourselves as spiritual leaders.

People simply do not follow someone for long who is not chasing a dream that is big and worthwhile. The drive to achieve financial targets cannot inspire people for too long. Even financial rewards are of limited use in motivating people. Spiritual leaders give direction to the energy. They turn up the energy all around them, an energy that sets others aflame. This energy is then allowed to flow through freely, making it easier for all to see the way to victory.

Why is a Strong Corporate Culture Not Enough?

Two aspects of corporate culture – being strong and healthy – must go hand-in-hand in order to achieve the desired synergy, as neither one of them alone could provide an adequate impetus to thoroughly fortify the company's entire immune system. There is a myth that acquiring a strong corporate culture is all it takes to safeguard the company against the woes of external viral attacks and provide sufficient insurance for its sustained long-term growth.

A strong corporate culture alone cannot insulate the company completely from the vagaries of the corporate environment and the onslaught of external viral attacks. One needs to build a healthy corporate culture that is action-oriented, based on the *yin* and interactive between the *yang* of the desired corporate philosophy and the free flow of internal energy. The over-reliance on a strong corporate culture can stifle and hinder the company from attaining its desired corporate objectives of continued long-term growth, as complacency sets in, creating a false sense of security and invincibility.

How Can One Change the Corporate Culture?

A powerful competitive tool in the 21st century is to establish an infrastructure for building a strong and healthy corporate culture. In the ever-competitive marketplace, many companies strive to differentiate their products or technology *vis-à-vis* their competitors in the hope of enlarging their market share. To achieve this end, much effort and resources are expended into acquiring superior technology or better marketing techniques. However, it is difficult to prevent competitors from quickly duplicating your technological advances, as well as your marketing ingenuity, since such tricks of the trade can be quickly emulated. But competitors will be unable to speedily replicate the success brought forth through a strong and healthy corporate culture, as it takes a long time to build one up. In fact, it is the most arduous and longest stage in the corporate turnaround process. To successfully develop this, the CEO must adopt a multi-pronged approach over a considerable length of time.

Someone mentioned that "Cultural change must come from the bottom and the CEO must guide it." This statement is totally true. How then can you change a culture from the top and yet ensure ownership down the line? The key lies in the fact that cultural change must be promulgated from the bottom of the organisational structure and the CEO can only guide its conception, development and dissemination. Therefore top management must initiate and lead the process while ownership must be thoroughly imbibed and "absorbed through osmosis" at the bottom, until the new corporate culture becomes fully integrated and internalised within the organisation. Building a strong and healthy immune system is not like having a one-time inoculation or even getting the occasional booster shots. It is more like taking vitamin pills every day for the rest of your life. How then can you change the company's corporate culture? The seven keys to changing the corporate culture are as follows:

1. Incorporate a healthy corporate philosophy/*qi*
2. Perform a gaps/needs assessment
3. Recruit change agents
4. Set the direction/goals
5. Change the processes/systems
6. Augment communication and training
7. Evaluate/measure the progress

EXERCISE 6.1
YOUR THERAPY STRATEGY, PART I

Consider what you need to put in place against each aspect of the Therapy Phase in order to maintain and support your company's turnaround.

Incorporating a new corporate philosophy	New ideas and ways of doing things	
	Acceptance of change as a constant	
	Willingness to accept failure as a result	
Free-flowing internal energy (Qi)	What is the current *qi* level in the company?	
	What should the future *qi* level be?	
	What impact will the *qi* level have on the future outlook of your products, markets and customers.	
A strong and healthy corporate culture	What is your 'cholesterol level'? Do you have too many 'bad' employees?	
	How do you use spiritual leadership?	
	Assess your progress against the 7 keys to corporate culture change: 1. Incorporate a healthy corporate philosophy/*qi* 2. Perform a gaps/needs assessment 3. Recruit change agents 4. Set the direction/goals 5. Change the processes/systems 6. Augment communication and training 7. Evaluate/measure the progress	

Productivity Measurements for Phase 3 Part 1

The "Therapy" phase implements the philosophy of seeking and embracing positive changes. This includes innovative process changes within the company: manufacturing or service processes, certainly, but also protocols related to human resources and employee development.

Some of the metrics in this phase should measure the continued improvements to previous productivity ratios. For example, let's revisit our old friend, the quality metric "manufacturing quality percentage", and check on his improvement:

- MQP (item count) ("MQP.IC"): (Total number of items produced minus number of defective items produced) divided by total number of items produced
- Change in MQP.IC: Current MQP.IC minus previous MQP.IC
- Growth in MQP.IC: (Current MQP.IC minus previous MQP.IC) divided by the previous MQP.IC

New productivity metrics are concerned with training, education and innovation. An example is:

- Educational investment per employee: Annual expenditure for education divided by the number of employees

Here are some of the productivity measurements to take during this phase:

1. Staff turnover: Number of resignations divided by the number of employees (head count)
   - During this phase, a reduction in staff turnover is desirable. If people are leaving due to dissatisfaction with the company, it indicates that the "Therapy" is not having its proper effect.
2. Financial productivity performance: Improvement in a productivity measurement divided by the expense of the productivity initiatives (dollars)
3. Annual gross innovations (**AGI**) per employee: Number of innovations suggested per year divided by the number of employees (head count)
   - These are productivity improvements, dealing with manufacturing or process efficiencies
4. Annual implemented innovations (**AII**) per employee: Number of innovations implemented per year divided by the number of employees (head count)
5. Increase in the annual gross innovations rate, based on #3 above: (Current AGI minus previous AGI), divided by previous AGI.
6. Increase in the annual implemented innovations (**AII**) rate, based on #4 above: (Current (**AII**) minus previous (**AII**)), divided by previous (**AII**)
7. Gross average value of recent innovations (**GAVRI**): Sales revenue (dollars) attributed to innovations introduced in the last year divided by the number of those innovations
8. Net average value of recent innovations: Profit (dollars) attributed to innovations introduced in the last year divided by the number of those innovations
9. Increase in the gross average value of recent innovations (**GAVRI**), based on #7 above: (Current GAVRI minus previous GAVRI), divided by previous GAVRI

10. Increase in the net average value of recent innovations (**NAVRI**), based on #8 above: (Current NAVRI minus previous NAVRI), divided by previous NAVRI

11. Gross investment in Research and Development (R&D) or innovations or productivity improvements, in dollars, as a percentage of gross revenue (**CRR**): Cost of all innovations divided by gross revenue

12. Change in gross investment in Research and Development (R&D) or innovations or productivity improvements (CRR): Current CRR minus previous CRR

13. Percentage increase in gross investment in Research and Development (R&D) or innovations or productivity improvements: (CRR): (Current CRR minus previous CRR), divided by previous CRR

14. Educational investment per employee (**EIE**) in a time period: Expenditure (dollars) for education, divided by the number of employees (head count)
    - If desired, the educational investment could be broken into categories: mentoring; formal in-house training; institutionalized training for specific skills; subsidies for general certifications or degrees such as MBA; and in-house educational resources such as books.

15. Change in the periodic educational investment per employee (**EIE**), based on #13 above: Current EIE minus previous EIE

16. Increase in the periodic educational investment per employee (**EIE**), based on #13 above: (Current EIE minus previous EIE), divided by previous EIE

17. Percentage of revenue spent on new product innovation (market research, technical research and development, planning marketing strategies, etc.) (**PCSI**): Cost of innovation (in dollars) divided by total revenue (in dollars)
    - This measurement was introduced in Phase 2.

18. Change in the percentage of revenue spent for new product innovation: Current PCSI minus previous PCSI

19. Growth of the percentage of revenue spent for new product innovation: (Current PCSI minus previous PCSI) divided by the previous PCSI

20. Percentage of employees receiving an educational investment (**EEI**): Number of employees receiving an educational investment divided by the total number of employees (head count)

21. Change in the percentage of employees receiving an educational investment: Current EEI minus previous EEI

22. Growth of the percentage of employees receiving an educational investment: (Current EEI minus previous EEI) divided by the previous EEI

23. Annual Number of "soft" process innovations researched or selected, per employee: Number of soft process innovations per year divided by the number of employees (head count)
    - These are changes to processes, like adding a suggestion box (or a suggestion tracking system) or instituting Six Sigma or 5S.

24. Percentage of revenue spent on "soft" process innovations (**SPI**): Cost of soft innovations (in dollars) divided by total revenue (in dollars)

25. Change in the percentage of revenue spent on "soft" process innovations (SPI): Current SPI minus previous SPI

26. Growth of the percentage of revenue spent on "soft" process innovations (SPI): (Current SPI minus previous SPI) divided by the previous SPI

27. Percentage of expenditure for new tools and equipment (dollars) compared to net book value of tools and equipment (dollars) (**NTE**): Expenditure for new tools and equipment (dollars) divided by net book value of tools and equipment (dollars)

28. Change in the percentage of expenditure for new tools and equipment (dollars) compared to net book value of tools and equipment (dollars): Current NTE minus previous NTR

29. Growth of the percentage of expenditure for new tools and equipment (dollars) compared to net book value of tools and equipment (dollars): (Current NTE minus previous NTE) divided by the previous NTE

30. A Staff Satisfaction Index (**SSI**) is an index which measures employee satisfaction and engagement in the workplace. Typically the HR department commissions an outside consulting firm to conduct an annual survey. Key success factors include: confidentiality; consistency in evaluating and reporting; high employee participation rate; and the analysis drills down to the department level (with a minimum number of employees in a "department" to ensure confidentiality). Upper management and HR may develop programs to train managers in the skills required to improve the SSI

Innovation Culture Measurements for Phase 3 Part 1

A successful and mature company uses established systematic processes to ensure the best outcomes in pursuing innovations.

Significant issues include: processes to improve quality; resources for innovation; rules that encourage innovation while maintaining high quality; and rewarding individual contributions toward innovation.

- Organizational Resources for Creativity:
    - o Does the organization provide facilities (office space, tools and equipment) dedicated for innovation?
    - o Does the organization provide a budget for innovation?
    - o Does the organization provide business information (strategic goals or market research) to the innovators?
- Individual Creativity:
    - o Do individuals regularly suggest innovations related to the marketing and selling of products?

Find the full set of questions in the **Innovation Culture in Ninety Questions** ™ tool.

END OF MODULE #6

The Therapy is under way. With a strong philosophy, your company's *Qi* is beginning to flow freely around the corporate body, embedding the new company culture. As the changes you are implementing begin to take widespread effect at every level of the company, it is time to take a look at another key factor in the corporate turnaround: office politics.

There is a saying about the business world, "It is a jungle out there." Is that true? If so, is it such a bad thing? Learn more in the office politics chapter.

~

XXXX ' Corporate Turnaround Centre

Additional Online Resources

The following book authored by Dr. Mike Teng is relevant to modules #6 and #8, covering the Therapy phase. Details are available by clicking on the website below.

Turnaround Handbook: Corporate Turnaround and Transformation
www.turnaroundhandbook.com

This is a very comprehensive handbook on corporate transformation and turnaround. It provides other online resources that the reader can turn to for guidance which includes ebooks, Youtube videos and poems on transforming the corporations. The handbook guides the reader on corporate transformation and turnaround at the strategic, tactical and individual levels.

You can also visit Dr. Mike Teng's www.youtube.com/1103teng **to watch related YouTube videos.**

It is time to change the way we think (Re-think Singapore)
http://tinyurl.com/rethinksingapore

Singapore, like many other countries, is going through a period of changes both in business structure and the economy. The global economy recession has forced us to re think the way that we use to earn a living. The rise of China and India has made it difficult for us to compete on prices for quality products and services. Our traditional markets in the West are decimated, and multi-national companies that we used to rely on for our domestic market are moving out. If we continue to rest on our past laurels, we will be doomed to failure. As matter of fact, our past successes are not workable anymore and we need to re-think, transform and turnaround if we are to survive and prosper going forward.

Turnaround, Transform Singapore

http://tinyurl.com/transformsingapore

The clarion call for the world economy and business environment is turnaround, transform and change. What has made Singapore successful in the past will not see us through the next five years as the business landscape has changed dramatically.

Turbulent times call for inspiring leaders

http://tinyurl.com/leaderinturbulenttimes

The failure to predict and address our current global financial problems could be directly attributed to poor leadership. It was bad and unprincipled leadership that brought us to the dismal situation we are in now. Fortunately, it will be good and principled leadership that can get us back on track again.

XXXX' Corporate Turnaround Centre

MODULE #7

OFFICE POLITICS /TEAMWORK

XXXX ' Corporate Turnaround Centre

"What we can learn from the animals about office politics"

If we look at our offices, and their political state
We can see lots of places, where we can seal our fate
Of losing out to that better dressed, better connected colleague
Who steals ideas and recognition, and plays in a different league

But if we look at the monkeys, who all work together
To bring in food for every one of them, to make them feel better
Here, they have a good idea, as they all profit well
From working for each other, no need to hard sell

The dogs and the cats, which we all grew up with
Made us happy through affection, and love they did give
They become another mouth to feed, but they were part of the family
But on them we need, to give them the best for prosperity

The wild dogs of this world have the right idea
When the lion has finished its meals, they suddenly appear
They don't have to hunt for food, as it's not a necessity
As they've learned to make the most of each opportunity

When we look at these animals, why do we call them dumb?
They've been showing us the way, almost from day one
They make the most of their skills, and they're personalities
To eat, gain love, and survive in the reality

Of a dog-eat-dog world, but with a fairness at heart
We too can learn from the beasts from the start
Have shown that with a little, genius and integrity
That we too can profit, and achieve prosperity

XXXX ' Corporate Turnaround Centre

INTRODUCTION

The animal world is rife with office politics and through simple observations, we can see how animals react to the same situations we find in the concrete jungle. The animals play politics as a way of life to survive in the jungle. And if they get played out, it may mean ending up as a meal for other animals. By making comparisons to the animal world, we can increase our toolbox of tactics to succeed in our offices. During these days of global economic slowdown, the political fight for job preservation becomes more intense, the ability to handle office politics is even more critical.

This is the rationale for this module. With the global recession, many jobs are going to be lost, and our concrete jungle is quickly becoming a true struggle for survival of the fittest. In these conditions, performance is not enough. By learning from animals that meet crisis frequently and observing how they survive, we can increase our own ability to survive in the concrete jungle.

This principle is universal, because as long as there are people, notwithstanding the culture, there are politics. We each must deal with people's egos, backgrounds and motivation (along with many other individual issues), and as jobs-retrenchment increases and companies go bust, the fight for job preservation and survival becomes increasingly intense. The animal behaviour in us surfaces in these circumstances. And when our animal behaviour increases, so does the tendency toward survival of the fittest.

When this type of behaviour takes precedence in the concrete jungle, everybody must wise-up and perform, otherwise he or she will not keep a job for very long. But simple performance under such circumstances is not enough. One needs to excel and stand out among the crowd - thus playing the political game well is critical.

XXXX ' Corporate Turnaround Centre

But playing well does not mean playing dirty. By no stretch of imagination am I espousing playing dirty politics. Animals do not do that, nor is it natural for humans to do so. Animals do not play the political game out of malice or greed. They play the game to protect themselves and their young. Even predators do not kill for killing's sake.

Once these predators have their fill, they leave the other prey-animals alone until the next meal. The animal ecosystem is a fair and balanced world that has lasted for millennia. This delicate balance based on ethical politics is why we do not see the systemic collapse of the animal kingdom as we are currently seeing in our economic system. The biggest destruction in the animal kingdom is actually caused by men who are invading into the animals' spaces, polluting the environment and the air, and hunting animals ruthlessly for private gain. Because of their delicate balance, the animals even survive the destructive forces of Mother Nature, such as drought and famine. But many species of animals are destroyed by men. It is in our best interest to learn from the animals and form this same balance in our lives to better survive in the concrete jungle.

Because the office environment really is "survival of the fittest" with a vicious and brutal life cycle - just as those boring books in science class described, keeping our wits about us in this setting is critical. And the pressure to do this has become more urgent in the face of the recent global economic downturn. This has led many people to consider how to best survive in this coming time which has already been rife with layoffs, mergers and general turmoil. After some very intriguing observations, I learned that there are some very strong similarities between the jungle and our offices. And that made me ponder the possibility that we might be able to learn some tricks from the animals to face the political game on our daily forays into the concrete jungle. Animals face crisis or the threat of crisis every day – from drought, famine, flood, forest fires to even being eaten alive if they're not careful enough. Animals have learned to cope with their own brand of office politics, honing their behaviour into a fine art of specialization for the survival of each of their species.

WAYS TO SUCCEED: BECOME KING OF THE JUNGLE

Standing out from the herd is critical if you want to lead, and is becoming more critical for simple survival in the economically distressed environment. In the jungle, the leader of the pack is chosen through feats of strength and posturing. In the office environment, battles are won in the same way.

Feats of strength are won or lost in an office, dependent on your position, tenure, the trust your partners have in you, and many other factors that are generally built up through years of playing the office politics game well. Simply put, this is because although in the jungle the animals can literally test each other, in the office, we simply cannot arm-wrestle every day to see who's the strongest (although it might be fun).

Posturing starts with carrying yourself with an air of leadership and thoughtfulness. And it's best if these characteristics are portrayed voluntarily and throughout your interactions with people. Assuming the mantle of authority by acknowledging others, teaching when the opportunity arises, and leading without being asked are the easiest and most gratifying ways to be recognized. Truly, when supervisors and co-workers look around the office for someone to be promoted or to lead important efforts, if you have consistently and voluntarily led for some time, the choice will be obvious. If you would take, you must first give; this is the beginning of intelligence.

The lion is the perfect animal-kingdom example to illustrate becoming king of the jungle – because he *is* the king of the jungle! The lion does occasionally play at exhibiting his strength through wrestling and aggressively defending his territory – don't think that I do not acknowledge this fact. However, much of his standing with the pack and much of why he only occasionally has to express his strength is posturing. The lion will spend much time marking his territory, sounding that deep-throated frightening roar and making that mane grow to an astonishing size.

By exhibiting these strong features and illustrating for the world to see that he is king, the lion convinces the den to let him lead, allowing him to choose when and where they will hunt.

So, what is the lion's first secret? Presentation. We've all heard the saying "Presentation is 99% of the work." Well, the saying is right. Many times, in the animal world, presentation is what it takes to convince another animal of strength or health, convincing the supposedly weaker to leave the resources to you. This is the same for humans – sometimes presentation is all it takes to convince someone that you're the best and should therefore get the praise.

The second most important tactic that the lion illustrates is that teaming-up is critical – and that never throwing his den-mates under the bus is a large part of that. The lion will make certain that each and every one of his den-mates have eaten before he stops hunting for the day – he needs his team to survive. Our offices are no different. We are dependent on one another for survival and must cultivate those relationships to ensure our individual success.

The final lesson from the king of the jungle is: Making shrewd and wise decisions based on knowledge can never harm your standing in the jungle!

WAYS TO FAIL – OFFICE MYTHS

There are many myths about office politics which can lead us to failure if we blindly follow them. And this is becoming more and more evident during this economically stressed time. If we cannot think beyond these old myths and learn to be flexible with the changing times, we are doomed to failure. So, what are these myths and how do we avoid them? If you try, surely you can think of some that may apply to your own career.

In my observations, there are five sure pitfalls that almost every one of us humans runs into throughout the course of our career:

1. **"If I just 'toe the party line' and stay loyal to my boss, I can't fail".**
2. **"I'm indispensable. They can't find fault with me"!**
3. **"I work hard – that's good enough".**
4. **"My boss loves me. Who cares if the other people in the office like me"!**
5. **"If I mind my own business, no one will bother me".**

Each of these dangerous attitudes can be assumed without you even knowing. They can be unconscious attitudes that grow from the tiny seed of being proud of one's accomplishments. But by taking a stance to monitor your attitudes and by looking to the potential for disaster, you can avoid even a hint of these undesirable stances. By looking at the way animals fail or flourish with these same attitudes, we might be able to make better decisions for long-term success.

XXXX ' Corporate Turnaround Centre

"If I just 'toe the party line' and stay loyal to my boss, I can't fail".

The myth that loyalty is all that you need to succeed has been debunked repeatedly in recent years. I have personally seen where many have failed because they assumed that the loyalty and devotion that they have provided their supervisor or mentor would be enough to carry them to success. If all you can see yourself doing is following the same person for the rest of your career, riding on the coattails of the ones before you, you're in trouble. This is a road to failure in so many instances.

Clearly, loyalty is not enough to sustain a career, and this is often also the case within the animal world. A faithful and loyal old wolf is still an old wolf in the eyes of the pack. When he is no longer useful and can no longer sustain himself, he will leave the pack and find a place to die. The same goes for many other animals – even domesticated cats and dogs. Most animals will either acknowledge that they are no longer contributing to the pack and leave, or if they are too saddled to know, then they are simply ushered out of the herd and left to die. Even bison will push the older, lamer members of the herd to the edges, sacrificing them to the predators while attempting to protect the young and virile in the centre of the herd.

To put it bluntly, no matter how long you have been around, nor how much loyalty you have shown, this is a "what have you done for me lately" world and you will not survive if there is not something more behind your loyalty. No boss will sustain a member of the team who is no longer contributing. Nor should you allow yourself to become that person. In these economically distressed times it will be evident who is pulling their weight and who is relying on only loyalty to survive. It is those people who will fall first to the layoffs and you want to avoid that at all costs.

XXXX ' Corporate Turnaround Centre

"I'm indispensable. They can't find fault with me"!

Avoiding overstepping one's boundaries is critical. This is a misstep that many a young manager or even seasoned executives take without sometimes realizing their folly. It is nice to believe that you are critical to an organization and it would make anyone feel good to truly be so important that no one would question your decisions; however, we are not invincible creatures. Even Steve Jobs was questioned for many years about his ability to run Apple – and although his is a good story now, time will only tell if his current empire will begin to crumble in the future. The ability we all have of making that assumption is inherent in our nature. We all strive to be the best, and it is wired in us to desire to attain that goal. But no one is perfect.

There is no good animal to point at to say "here's how the animal world is cruel to its own that overstep their bounds" - because there is not. The alligator knows that it cannot kill the hippopotamus. The lion knows that to take the whole herd of bison down is very unwise. The snake even knows that to take on a dog or a cat is a last-defence. No animal is invincible. Every animal is vulnerable, and we people are the same in all our life choices, including office politics.

"I work hard – that's good enough".

Hard work is only a basic building block of success within today's corporate world. The rules that guide us demand that we not only work hard, but that good results be produced accordingly. If we cannot focus on many items, including working hard, we might as well quit now, because we're simply wasting time.

Many birds work for weeks to build a nest. However, often they must leave the nest to find food, if even for just a moment. But while the nest is alone, it is vulnerable and can be easily destroyed by an invading snake looking to loot for eggs. The lesson that we can learn from the birds is to keep our work from

215

being fruitless and empty by protecting the investments we have made. You do this not by just working hard, but working the political game and winning.

"My boss loves me. Who cares if the other people in the office like me"?

Your boss is only your boss as long as he doesn't find another job, gets promoted or gets transferred. Tomorrow someone else in your office could just as easily be your boss as your current boss. Additionally, management comes and goes with mergers and acquisitions. If you bet the wrong horse, you will be cast out with the old horses. And I don't recommend that you test it in these economically difficult times. Too many people have learned this lesson too late in their careers to start again, and they found themselves stuck with a new set of supervisors.

All we must do is to look at the cockroach to prove that this myth is a dangerous one to believe. The cockroach is well-built, with an exoskeleton that is virtually indestructible. The cockroach is designed to safely get through some of the roughest environmental times. They may even be able to out-live a nuclear holocaust! But the cockroach has one very big drawback – they are just gross! The cockroach is a despicably nasty little creature living in darkness and breeding in massive quantities. It is obvious by the significant numbers of baby cockroaches that they love each other. But no one else likes them. The lesson we can learn is that while we might feel the love of our boss, certainly, if we become anything like the cockroach, certainly someone should be coming after us with a can of bug-spray, too!

The lesson is a hard one, but one we should all heed. At no time should we consider that we are better than our co-workers, because they could just as easily be the new favourite tomorrow as we are today.

"If I mind my own business, no one will bother me".

This myth is very true. If you sit at your desk and work without becoming involved in the office environment around you, you will slowly rot. Or, you will be unprepared, vulnerable to attack and eaten alive. Having no one bother you equates to: No one will bother with you. Being quiet and ignoring the outside world is a recipe for being forgotten and passed over for the things that you want. So, don't fade into the background – learn to stand out!

Just like we should do in the concrete jungle, animals walk cautiously in the jungle. They mind their businesses – but they interact with the other animals significantly, observing their surroundings and observing the actions of the animals around them. By running from danger, the deer can lessen the likelihood that they will become the meal.

This is so applicable to the corporate world! And as a successful executive, you must know it better than everyone else that you have to constantly keep moving to stay ahead of others!

XXXX ' Corporate Turnaround Centre

Office Political Situations During The Three Phases

	Surgery: Famine time	Resuscitation: New pastures	Therapy: Innovation Watering hole
Bosses	1. Eat their young 2. Killer instinct	1. Look for new areas 2. Pack leader	1. Share their kill 2. Co-exist with other animals
Colleagues	1. Assertive skills 2. Survival of the fittest	1. Presentation skills 2. Bring in new skills	1. Social skills 2. Sharing the excesses
Corporate Culture	1. No waste 2. Alert of other predators and even own species	1. Moving out to new feeding ground 2. Watch for other predators	1. Breeding session 2. Take care of the young

XXXX ' Corporate Turnaround Centre

EXERCISE 7.1
BUSTING YOUR MYTHS

STAGE ONE:

These dangerous attitudes can lead to your downfall or prevent your success. Be honest with yourself. Which of them do you suffer from?

"If I just 'toe the party line' and stay loyal to my boss, I can't fail".
Loyalty is not enough; what are you doing to ensure your survival?

"I'm indispensable. They can't find fault with me"!
The most dispensable person is the one that thinks they are indispensable. When have you fallen into the trap of believing you are perfect?

"I work hard – that's good enough".
Do you neglect your image and exposure because you think working hard is all that is important?

"My boss loves me. Who cares if the other people in the office like me"?
Is your success based on you or on the person who supports you? Do you need a wider network of colleagues?

"If I mind my own business, no one will bother me".
Do you have presence? Do you stand out or are you part of the office furniture?

STAGE TWO:

Now ask yourself, what do I need to do to play the office politics game better?

CONCLUSION

No matter how many tools are in your toolbox or sources of income you have, you will not always know the right move to make or the right stance to take. No single stance will always be the right political stance. The key lesson here is to learn from the animals, take the information they can give you, and put it to your use.

For example, bears hibernate in winter, but store-up great amounts of fat to make it through those lean months. From them we can learn to build up good will with our co-workers even during the good times, so that in the bad times we have more good-will backlog. And we can learn that saving can be the key to surviving economic difficulties, so we should always be working toward increasing our savings.

Another example would be the eagle. Eagles soar *with* the wind and not against it, making the most of the fickle breezes to carry them high to find prey. The eagle will not fight the wind, knowing that to do so would force him to plummet to the ground.

Likewise, we should accept, gracefully, any uplift that comes to us throughout our career. We should use the opportunities that are presented to us, even if they might not be exactly what you desire at the moment.

Every animal will have something to teach us, be it something small that might influence a single interaction or something significant that could influence one's entire career. We need to read into what the animal's tactics are to learn the valuable lessons they can share.

Acknowledge that we all need to work on our personal development and take the lessons the animals can give us and then improve ourselves. Know the situation and move with the tides. Adapt with the changing circumstances and situations. Determine the specific issues, problems and then determine the appropriate solutions. No problem is so great that it cannot be overcome – and there are many solutions.

We should each review the experience of the last Great Depression when jobs were dropping like dead flies – performance is not enough. One must impress everyone around you so that you will be one of the last few standing. To do this, we can learn from the animals in times of drought and famine. The rule of survival of the fittest is truly evident in the animal world during drought and famine. The same can be said for the corporate jungle during times of economic difficulty. The fittest in the corporate jungle are those that know how to impress quickly and are able to perform consistently.

To ensure that you will be one of the fittest and survive, especially if your firm is hurting during these financially unstable markets, you can manage your office politics tactics by modifying them to better suit the changing culture of the office. Changes in the market mandate change for yourself and your firm. For example, if your firm is facing an upturn in profits but a significant overage in workload, you can change your stance to better handle this change (although this might be unusual in our economy today). Or if your office is having a slow-down in the workload and the culture is changing to increase the amount of marketing necessary to win a project, to survive, you must change too.

The same can be said for changes to the political environment in your office. The changes in the economy have caused many managers to become much more hands-on, stripping responsibilities from young professionals in an effort to ensure quality. If you are one of these young professionals, you must change with this change in your office's political culture. If you are one of the managers, you must acknowledge this change in your peers and determine if you will make this change, or if you will buck the system. Either way, you will need to change the behaviour you have toward your peers and your young professionals. Any way you look at it, you must modify yourself and your behaviour to deal with a change in the office politics environment around you. But first you must open your mind and understand that you are the only one who can influence your career in such a significant manner. By learning from the animals that change can benefit you, you can become a better office politics player.

"Surviving office politics"

Whether you are in demand, or on the bottom rung
Whether you are in command, or having no fun
You have to understand, that there are certain tricks
To surviving the world, of office politics

It is not very easy, when everything seems so wrong
It gets harder and harder, to do dance to the song
When you know you are better, than the guy above
He only has the job, because his hand fits the CEO's glove

It can be hard to stay focused, when you are being put down
It can be hard to work hard, when your face is on the ground
But there are lessons to learn, that will help you survive
In the mad world of politics, play the game right and it will keep you alive

Don't be too hasty, to muscle in on the action
Don't be too pushy, or you may just be a faction
And easily lost, or pushed out the door
You'll end up on your ass, sitting alone on the floor

XXXX' Corporate Turnaround Centre

END OF MODULE #7

We have used the animal world as a metaphor and classroom and learned some valuable lessons about what goes on in our offices. Understanding human (and *animal*!) dynamics within your workforce is crucial to effectively implementing the Therapy Phase of your turnaround. In the next module, we return to the key stages of your company's therapy. It will be time for more action!

~

XXXX ' Corporate Turnaround Centre

Additional Online Resources

The following books authored by Dr. Mike Teng are relevant to this module, covering office politics. Details are available by clicking on the website below for each book.

What we can learn from the animals about office politics: How to play in the concrete jungle without being played out

www.officepolitic.com

Often, playing office politics can make you feel like you are navigating in a dangerous jungle, jumping one obstacle only to discover that a predator is on your tail. It's no wonder that the animals that navigate the real jungle might have some insight for us office-predators and office-prey.

Office Politics Mania

www.officepoliticsmania.com

This is a book using cartoons to illustrate the craziness of things taking place in the offices today. It helps reader to laugh over the realities of the office politics.

You can also visit Dr. Mike Teng's www.youtube.com/1103teng **to watch the YouTube videos of some of the books.**

Office politics mania

http://tinyurl.com/officepoliticsmania

We are watching too many corporate executives and owners of businesses develop ulcers, or worse, experience heart problems. Many people feel overwhelmed by financial burdens and fighting office politics to survive. We all seek relief. Rest assured that this video has sincerely stepped forth to ease your pain! Let's face it: the trauma created by this crisis appears to be just as present in Singapore as it is in Los Angeles, can we all agree? And office mania is prevalent all over.

How to play office politics without being played out

http://tinyurl.com/officepolitics1

Have you ever asked yourself the question: Are office politics really that bad? And found yourself answering "Yes"! Well, perhaps this is the book for you. Dr. Mike Teng, author of a best-selling book "Corporate Turnaround: Nursing a sick company back to health" creates a unique and delightful view into the world of office politics. He vividly illustrates how we can refocus our energies from viewing office politics as a bad thing provided those same politics are played fairly and as a part of life and natural!

What can we learn from the Animals about Office Politics?

http://tinyurl.com/officepolitics2

Are you struggling to deal with office politics AGAIN?! Have you tried all the tactics you can think of to succeed in this rough economic depression only to find yourself on the chopping block? Unemployment rates in the U.S. are surging to rise well above the highest level that they have been in 20+ years! And in Europe, the numbers are staggeringly similar. In this kind of global economic crisis, your job is at stake every day.

MODULE #8

–

PHASE THREE (Cont'd):
THERAPY Part II

AN ACTION-DRIVEN ORIENTATION

An important component of the strong and healthy corporate culture is embracing an action-driven orientation. The turnaround CEO must strive to convince the staff to discard the old mentalities and in their place embrace the flexibility, speed and innovation of its action-driven orientated culture.

- **Flexibility** in the corporate culture, facilitating smooth adaptation to changes
- **Fast** and first in implementation of the right operational strategy, and
- **Innovation** in getting creative and good ideas implemented successfully and profitably

Flexible and Fast to Win

Today, opportunities come and go at fast speed. Economic integration has blown open protected markets. Deregulation has torn down monopolies. The Internet has changed the bricks and mortar into millstones. Life cycles of products, strategies, and business advantages are getting shorter. Businesses need to be fast and nimble-footed to adapt instantly to changing market conditions. In effect, it includes being fast and always trying to be first whenever possible. This concept of flexibility is also mentioned by Sun Tzu: "The guiding principle in military tactics may be likened to water. Just as flowing water avoids the heights and hastens to the lowlands, an army should avoid strengths and strike weaknesses."

An example of a company that thrives on the fast and flexible model is Hewlett-Packard (HP). HP continues its transformation journey under its CEO Mark Hurd, from an underperforming printer-reliant giant into the world's largest tech company, whose business is thriving in multiple markets. In 2009, HP surpassed Dell as the top PC seller and, in the process, showed Apple-worthy design chops with its sleek "TouchSmart" computers featuring touchscreen functionality. HP's $2.7 billion acquisition of 3Com -- a year after the $13 billion deal for EDS made it an instant IBM & Cisco rival.

Innovation to recreate and rejuvenate

Company needs to build an innovative culture. Many successful discoveries were founded because innovators asked questions. An example is the invention of the shipping container, resulting in the modern-day container port that accelerated the growth of world trade. The founder asked questions as to how he can improve the transportation of goods in an effective and efficient manner. He learned it from the military which transports in standard size containers to carry military equipment overseas for war. Other innovative products were founded because the innovators were observing and exploring. Examples included the discovery of contraceptive pill and Barbie doll. The founders were experimenting and looking for new things. Innovators also network and allow ideas to flow freely. The game Scrabble was founded on this basis because the founder created the game and started to share, network and improve the game. Innovators also vision. This was the basis of the assembly line when Henry Ford was visioning and looking for a system to automate the production of the automobiles. The assembly line concept revolutionises the modern-day manufacturing.

Conversely, an innovative culture can be destroyed because top management is suspicious of every idea that originated from rank and file. Top management become bureaucratic to insist people go through different levels with a new idea. They are critical and withhold praise as well as controlling and organising in secret. Such behaviours and attitudes will destroy the innovative spirit in the organisations.

An Action-Driven Orientation: Cheaper, Better and Faster

Even in this phase, management still must be oriented toward action rather than introspection or complacency.

Cheaper: Foster a culture that looks for savings without sacrificing quality. In fact, investing in higher quality tends to reduce overall costs. That includes both "higher quality of input materials" and "improving the quality of internal processes."

Better: In difficult economic times, some customers will try to save a bit by buying lower-quality goods or services. Most, however, will choose an item of higher quality for the same price. Even the price-conscious consumer may turn to a higher-quality brand when they can afford it. Always try to improve the quality of your products or services; the competitive advantages outweigh the burden.

Faster: The emphasis here is to minimize the time it takes to bring an innovation to the marketplace. This allows your company to set market expectations in terms of base product, quality, features, pricing, and follow-up service.

EATING A BALANCED DIET

The balanced diet that will ward off the corporate doctor is: **Vision** for breakfast, **Feedback** for lunch and **Action** for dinner. Any break or disruption in the balanced diet can seriously hamper the company's operations and derail its quest towards continued long-term growth.

Vision and Feedback without Action – Dreaming

Many multinational companies have excellent vision. There are also some that are too slow or inflexible in their actions, resulting in lost opportunities or making the right decision too late. No strategy is worth much if it is not translated into concrete action for implementation. It is imperative to ensure that every business and supporting unit has a plan that it can execute in sync with the overall corporate strategy

Action without Vision and Feedback – Wasting Time

On the other hand, the extreme of concentrating on action alone is often adopted by many companies. They over-diversify into numerous ventures and acquisitions at break-neck speed without judicious evaluations as to whether they complement their corporate objectives and market feedback. So goes the adage: "Fail to plan and you plan to fail." Consequently, many of these companies suffer massive losses from their bad decisions.

Vision, Feedback, Action – Keeping the Corporate Doctor Away

We need all three meals – Vision, Feedback and Action. In Module #6 we discussed the power of *qi* or internal energy. These internal energies will not be harnessed and exploited if no action or decision is taken. This is why Sun Tzu said: "Energy may be likened to the bending of a crossbow; decision, to the releasing of a trigger."

There is a saying that information is power. Some claim that it should be knowledge that is power, as knowledge is basically the relevant information sifted through feedback that is useful to the vision and goals of the company.

However, both information and knowledge are useless if no one utilises them.

It is similar to the treatment of a sick patient. The doctor can have all the right information as well as knowledge on how to cure the patient; however, if he does not take the suited action for the treatment, it is of no use. Conversely, action has to be complemented with the correct information and knowledge. Acting on the wrong information and knowledge may kill the patient.

This is why all three – Vision, Feedback and Action are required. It is the "Application of correct information and knowledge" that is power. In the context of management theory, it is useful to apply the best blend of Eastern and Western styles. There is no doubt that "Developing Asia" can learn a lot from the more established and intellectual Western management theory. Of particular superiority are areas pertaining to professional management, incorporating the merits of clear vision, proper research techniques, feedback and analysis. However, the West can learn from the Asian instinctive and entrepreneurial abilities to quickly act upon information available.

Put in the proper perspective, "Vision and Feedback without Action" is daydreaming while "Action without Feedback" is a waste of time. All three must work collectively to achieve the synergistic results of reinforcing a strong and healthy corporate culture that will propel the company towards continued long-term growth.

ACTIVE COMMUNICATION

Oftentimes, relationships break down because of poor communication. When communication breaks down, it results in misunderstanding, rumour-mongering, negative comments (or verbal diarrhoea) and finally ill health.

Similarly in the company, when communication breaks down, the rapport, metabolism and chemistry of the people suffer. The doctor examines the tongue to determine the general health of the patient. The tongue is the organ used by the body for communication and can determine the morale level and state of mental health of the company by examining the manner of communication. In sick companies, negative comments and rumours will abound.

Communication is one of the cornerstones supporting the new corporate culture during the Therapy phase. To strengthen and nurture this, the turnaround CEO needs to create a culture marked with candour and straight talk. In the modern world, market information and ideas are precious and highly perishable commodities that need to be speedily exploited and acted upon in order to fully harness their value. Therefore, the organisational structure needs to be informal and non-hierarchical, with non-verbal communication being consistent with the verbal ones, and it is necessary to communicate frequently, as well, at all levels.

Unlike in Phase I where the communication style tends to be close and didactic, Phase III calls for a more open and interactive style. Phase III communication entails the following:
- Informal and non-hierarchical structure
- Non-verbal communication
- Frequent communication at all levels

Informal and Non-hierarchical Structure

Since timeliness is of the essence, communication lines must be kept short and direct. Always pare protocol by encouraging informality and allowing quick access to market information, which can then be acted upon swiftly and flexibly.

Non-verbal Communication

The non-verbal aspects of communication are often more important than the verbal ones. Consider ideas such as all members of the team sharing an open-plan office with the same kind of furniture and also shared secretarial services. This "flat" and informal management style is similar to that which project teams use to get a job done effectively and efficiently. It is also a style that allows for maximum interaction and feedback. Such style also demonstrates to the staff members that everybody is of equal importance to the organisation. This principle demands that there be no visible isolation of the CEO, senior managers and the junior staff. The management can be easily accessible which is so critical to facilitate communication. It also releases the internal energy, or *qi*, of the staff.

Frequent Communication at All Levels

In addition to non-hierarchical and informal communication, the turnaround CEO needs to frequently communicate at every opportunity. You cannot simply communicate with a few hundred people at the top and expect change to occur. You may have to doggedly repeat the key messages over and over again using every opportunity to reinforce them.

Conscious efforts should be made to utilise all possible channels to communicate with the staff: at formal gatherings, training sessions, meetings, team briefings and even informal get-togethers. These are excellent opportunities to foster a strong culture, as staff members are receptive and need to feel good about working in a good corporation. They are given clear messages and expectations on the desired corporate image, market orientation and employee attitudes.

Leaders energise others when they personally interact with them and the enthusiasm can then be passed on and eventually be infused within the organisation.

Thus, during this therapy phase, the basic aim of the communication system is twofold. One is to clearly disseminate the management's message to all levels in the organisation while fostering trust and openness as well. In this way, the free flow of internal energy, ideas, opinions and feedback will engineer fast speed and flexibility in action. The statement, "Leaders communicate the corporate culture and help others to achieve it", captures the essence of communication during Phase III.

A POSITIVE MENTAL ATTITUDE

In addition to eating and communicating well, the turnaround CEO needs to inculcate a positive mental attitude to strengthen the immune system of the organisation. As Willie Nelson, singer and song writer, said, "Once you replace negative thoughts with positive ones, you will start having positive results."

What makes Homo sapiens (human beings) different from other living creatures is primarily the mental attitude. Doctors have long recognized the placebo effect where patients react just as strongly to sugar pills as to the real thing. Hypnotists have demonstrated the power of the mind to control pain and afflictions to the body. By changing their mental attitude, some patients stricken with heart diseases or even cancer have actually dissipated such diseases from their systems. Positive mental attitude originates in the non-verbal parts of the brain, which also interacts with the body systems that control the blood pressure and immune responses. When your mental attitude is negative, you have chronic, hopeless and depressed feelings that drive the immune system into a "self-destructive mode" where viruses can easily establish a foothold. A positive mental attitude includes the following:

- Preparing for succession
- Enhancing professional image
- Improving employee attitude

- Encouraging rest and recreation

Preparing for Succession

History has demonstrated the fall of many countries because of poor succession of leadership. Yugoslavia plunged into civil war in 1980 with the demise of the once all-powerful President Tito, who had no intention of passing control of power to anybody.

Poor succession-planning is also one of the major causes of failures among many companies. This is because many companies – especially family-owned businesses – find it mentally difficult to pass the helm of control to outsiders and professional managers. The owners want to pass the business down to their offspring who may have no interest or capability to take over. It is a negative mental attitude because these owners do not want to lose control of the company to outsiders. However, in the long run, it is more beneficial to the company, as well as to the owners and their offspring, to have the best person to run the business. The best person or successor in many instances may not be their offspring. This is why there is a Chinese saying: "The first generation builds the business, the second generation enjoys the prosperity and growth and it will be squandered away and decline by the third generation."

Enhancing the Professional Image

The professional image consists of two parts, namely the corporate image and the customer-driven orientation. While corporate image deals with the more overt signs and icons which can be readily implemented, for instance, corporate colours, brochures, uniforms, dress code, name tags and calling cards. However, the customer-driven orientation aspects are more subtle and exacting. The former is critical, as customers form impressions about the organisation very quickly through what they see. Oftentimes, you do not have a second chance to impress them. The latter usually demands a fundamental shift in the mindset of the staff towards providing better customer service.

Improving Employee Attitude

Another element of paramount importance to strengthening the immune system is improving employee attitude. It is often said that "the difference between heaven and hell is not the altitude but the attitude." Throughout the corporate turnaround process, small changes in the staff's mindset can reap long strides in boosting the health of the corporate culture within the organisation. Every little success is recognised, commended and celebrated. It is partly psychological. Once people start to achieve success, it spurs them on to greater efforts. Credit is accorded to the staff when due, such as public recognition, awarding of certificates of appreciation and plaques. Such little gestures and encouragement produce the glue that cement the fabric of the corporate culture and solidify efforts made in rehabilitating the company.

Eventually, a resilient and robust corporate culture will evolve and be entrenched within the company. This legacy benefits not only the company that is being successfully turned around. but also the individual employees. The impact of such changes in values is highly rewarding and cannot be quantified in monetary terms. The sense of pride derived from such an extraordinary experience is indescribable. This experience may be similar to that felt by a doctor when he manages to heal a gravely ill patient. Indeed, the turnaround CEO's sense of achievement is complete when he is able to render this magical elixir or touch of injecting life into a perishing company and rescue it from the brink of disaster and certain death.

Encouraging Rest and Recreation

One of the most effective ways to de-stress and improve mental health is rest and recreation. People also produce their best results when they are relaxed and comfortable at their workplace. Nothing relaxes people more than rest and recreation.

Rest

The first concept of rest in the corporate context is stability. There is a paradox here. To cope with the rapid changes, the company needs to change. However, in the quest for growth-inducing changes, the company also needs rest and stability. This is the same principle as a human body needing rest for the body to re-charge and repair itself but at the same time the human body needs to be active in order to achieve optimal body functions and good health. This is why the turnaround managers have to master the art of preserving stability amidst change as well as spurring change during stability. By the third phase, your management team should be established and major restructuring is needed only when necessary.

Some companies hire and fire whenever they like. This is binge-and-purge staffing or corporate bulimia[13]. Such frequent changes in management and staff not only breed suspicion and disloyalty among the staff but can also destroy the fabric of corporate cohesion and *esprit de corps*. Self-interest replaces corporate interest as loyalty and trust are lost. This is why during the Therapy stage, one has to address the "soft" issues and stabilise the operations in order to sustain long-term growth.

Recreation

"All work and no play, makes Jack a dull boy." So goes the adage. Though employees work hard to earn a living, they also have social needs that can be met at the workplace through recreation. If the work is perceived to be fun, enjoyable and relaxing, even mundane chores seem bearable and people will put their hearts and souls into their jobs. People need recreation because human beings are generally social animals. Recreation gives them a chance to relax from the tedium and tensions of work life, as well as an opportunity to

---

[13] An illness in which there is a great and uncontrollable desire to eat, usually followed by vomiting in order not to gain weight.

bond with their colleagues. As a result, they can also become a lot more creative and co-operative.

Proper support and feedback can be obtained from the staff at such recreational events rather than formal meetings. It is through such times that relationships are cemented. CEOs and managers can show their genuine involvement in the life of the company by taking recreational and informal participation more seriously. For instance, showing up at company's sports events such as soccer games, bowling and golf tournaments will not have the same impact as playing in them together with the staff. This is because the latter provides opportunities for the staff to establish the rapport with their management.

EMPHASISING EXERCISE
(Training and Development)

Training and development are like physical exercises that help the body to generate endorphins[14] which give a sense of well-being, helping it to cope with stress and other ailments. Endorphins are internally-produced painkillers that help pregnant mothers-to-be to go through the pains of child-delivery and fathers-to-be to weather the storms of a job loss. Physical exercise or gymnastics also promotes top-form agility, flexibility and mobility.

Employees need to be motivated to make contributions to the unit that transcends their job description. They need to use their brains and hearts, in addition to their hands. Fostering such behaviour requires not only the right culture of trust, but also incentives, training and development.

Delegation of even more complex decisions can only be successful if employees are given the chance to grow their knowledge and skills with the challenges. Asking employees to go beyond the call of duty or beyond their standard job descriptions in their employment contract requires giving them the opportunity to advance themselves and their careers. Everyone has untapped potential that can be nurtured within the right environment. We can reap significant contributions with appropriate training and development:
- Transform the mindset
- Engender a quality service culture
- Act as a catalyst for change

Training and development are effective change tools to facilitate the engendering of a healthy corporate culture during the nursing phase. This is a highly controversial subject, as some feel that it is a waste of resources to

---

[14] Substances produced by the brain that have a similar effect as morphine.

train staff who may eventually resign. However, there is a fallacy in such an argument, as companies really cannot afford not to train their staff. Companies will invest millions on machinery and equipment, but some stint on investing in their most important assets – their people. Investing in people pays dividends in the long term. A patient with kidney disease would not entrust the treatment of his ailment to a general practitioner, knowing fully that it requires treatment from a specialist. Likewise, unless the top management wants to risk the onset of a corporate kidney failure, it should ensure that the company's staff members are adequately trained for their jobs. Employees need "topping up", retraining and new training throughout their careers.

Transform the Mindset

Noel M. Tichy, author of "*The Leadership Engine*", said, "The key to winning today and to creating an organisation that can win again tomorrow, is teaching. If you look at the world's best leaders, you will see that they are also the world's best teachers, because teaching is at the heart of leadership." Jack Welch, for example, takes training and development very seriously. He spent a lot of time in his later years at General Electric (GE) coaching and teaching his younger colleagues, transforming their mindsets.

Engender a Quality Service Culture

Singapore Airlines (SIA) is another world-class company that emphasizes the importance of training and development. Dr. Cheong Choong Kong, CEO of SIA, on the airline's training philosophy, said: "Training is a necessity, not an option. It is not to be dispensed with when times are bad. Training is for everybody. It embraces everyone from the office assistant and baggage handler to the managing director. We do not skimp on training. We'll use the best in software and hardware that money can buy. Because we take a long-term view of training, our investments in staff development are not subject to the vagaries of the economy. Training is forever. No one is too young to be trained, nor too old." SIA opened an S$80 million (US$46 million) training centre in 1993. Today, SIA still conducts rigorous training and retraining that builds a powerful service culture.

Wal-Mart is expert at using core competencies to become superior to their competitors. There are three resources which allow a company to create a core competency. Tangible resources consist of assets that can be seen, financial resources (borrowing capacity), physical resources, organizational structure and technology. Wal-Mart is a huge and very powerful company and therefore uses its ability of lending to become a core competency. Intangible resources are characterized by human resources, resource for innovation, and reputation. This category is where Wal-Mart excels against all its competitors. Knowledge, training and corporate culture possessed by employees may be one of the most significant sources of core competencies and competitive advantages throughout the business world. This is due to being very hard to copy or substitute for. Brand equity consists of brand name and maintaining brand equity. Wal-Mart is a master at using this resource as an advantage over the competitors.

IBM (International Business Machines) spends over $700 million per year on training, and the average employee gets 54 hours of training per year. The Armonk, NY-based giant was cited as an innovator, with programs such as an $85 million learning initiative for managers and executives. Pfizer spends 14 percent of its overall budget on training, including its new Retaining Knowledge program, which helps senior leaders who are changing jobs to transfer knowledge and skills to successors.

Act as a Catalyst for Change

Training is crucial in generating grassroots ideas and initiatives that fuelled turnaround efforts in some companies. To reinforce the training mentality, every training session is utilised as a message platform. Though requiring perseverance, such reinforcements will reap the desired results in the long run.

This entire process should be spearheaded by selecting a team of core change-agents. They could include selected staff within the company or external parties engaged to act as facilitators.

PEOPLE, PEOPLE and PEOPLE

Businesses provide consumers with goods and services. Businesses consist of machinery and equipment run by people. Business creativity and productive capacity come from the ability of its people. Therefore, people are the business's most important assets. The value of human resources cannot be under-estimated in creating a strong and healthy corporate culture to sustain long-term growth. Every company will have to rely on its employees to bring in the business. They form the foundation of the company. As the business world evolves to embrace the information technology environment or knowledge based economy, a company must never forget that it is people who form the core of its corporate assets. How these highly qualified employees are handled by the management is extremely crucial, as their departure can severely cripple the company's operations.

The great Chinese philosophers also emphasise taking care of people. The philosopher, Mencius (371–289 BC), recommended reward to ensure that in both good and bad times, the people do not worry about their livelihood and will follow their leader. Tao Zhu-gong also recognised this and said that people must be handled cordially. "An irritable temper and bad attitude will diminish sales greatly." Just as a company expects an employee to be loyal, it too must be loyal to the employee. Indeed, the Chinese character for loyalty, *zhong*, contains two words, *zhong* which means centre and *xin* which means heart. Loyalty therefore means that the central focus is on the heart of the employees. Once you win over their hearts and souls, you have their loyalty.

EXERCISE 8.1

YOUR THERAPY STRATEGY, PART II

Continue to consider what you need to put in place against each aspect of the Therapy Phase in order to maintain and support your company's turnaround.

An action-driven orientation	_Flexibility_ of the corporate culture	
	Fast implementation of the right operational strategy	
	Focus on core competence	
Eat a balanced diet	Vision – do you know where you are going?	
	Feedback – do you have the right information?	
	Action – do you take the right action?	
Active communication	Do you have an informal and non-hierarchical structure?	
	Do you implement non-verbal communication?	
	Is there frequent communication at all levels?	
Cultivating a positive mental attitude	Do you have a succession plan?	
	How are you enhancing the professional image?	
	What steps have you taken to measure and improve employee attitude?	
	How do you encourage rest and recreation?	
Emphasising exercise	How do you influence and reinforce the positive mindset of your managers?	
	How do you use training and development to engender a quality service culture?	
	How does training and development act as a catalyst for change?	
People, people, and people	How does your company demonstrate its loyalty to its people?	

XXXX' Corporate Turnaround Centre

Innovation Culture Measurements for Phase 3 Part 2

The organization must provide resources and an infrastructure to support innovation.

Management must lead by example, by pro-actively seeking and developing new opportunities.

Individual attempts should be honoured, even if they do not result in immediate success. Successes should be celebrated and rewarded.

Some questions to ask are:

- Does the organization's infrastructure meet the needs of the employees?
- Does management address initiatives proposed by individuals?
- Does the organization follow a process to learn from a failure?
- Does management reward the performance of individuals?

Find the full set of questions in the **Innovation Culture in Ninety Questions ™** tool.

END OF MODULE #8

Your Therapeutic Strategy is complete and the Therapy has begun. With a balanced corporate diet of vision, feedback and action, your company's communication is improving and the professional image and attitudes are aligned to your success. Your commitment to training and development is demonstrating your loyalty to your most important asset: your people. In the next module we take an overview of the medical and spiritual metaphors and the turnaround process by looking at Corporate Wellness. Topics include disease prevention, diagnosis, treatment, recovery and strengthening.

~

Additional Online Resources

The following book authored by Dr. Mike Teng is relevant to modules #6 and #8, covering the Therapy phase. Details are available by clicking on the website below.

You can also visit Dr. Mike Teng's www.youtube.com/1103teng to watch relevant YouTube videos.

Turbulent times call for inspiring leaders

http://tinyurl.com/leaderinturbulenttimes

The failure to predict and address our current global financial problems could be directly attributed to poor leadership. It was bad and unprincipled leadership that brought us to the dismal situation we are in now. Fortunately, it will be good and principled leadership that can get us back on track again.

MODULE #9

CORPORATE WELLNESS

INTRODUCTION

Medical and spiritual metaphors are used abundantly in this module as I believe that people can comprehend their financial conditions much better than corporate matters. Metaphor is a comparative figure of speech in which a term is transferred from the object it ordinarily designates to an object it may designate only by implicit comparison or analogy. It is a comparison of something familiar to something unfamiliar and used in this module to explain a common "corporate wellness" principle. It is an effective way for people to create meaning by using one element of experience to understand another. Or to use an analogy, metaphor is like a bridge, it spans the gap between what the turnaround manager wants the sick company to know and what the sick company already knows.

Metaphor gives us the opportunity to stretch our imagination, create powerful insights and deepen our understanding, thereby allowing us to see and act in new ways. Such metaphors couched into principles serve to enable the executives to draw parallels to their corporate issues and facilitate their diagnosis and remedies.

There are many similarities between a company and a person. Just like a human being, a company can get ill. Many companies are falling sick due to a whole host of factors such as the economic slowdown, competition and incompetent management. Sickness is a big business but nobody wants to *be* the patient or *remain* as the patient. Corporate ill health is also a big business, as in a declining and stagnant economy like the economic conditions we experienced in late 2008; there were more sick companies than healthy ones. Every company and individual wants to be in the pink of health.

It is important to keep your body healthy and well. Doctors generally only treat the disease and do not treat wellness. Individuals are beginning to recognize the importance of commercialized health which is becoming a big business.

The pharmaceutical industry understands this as the drugs consumed for surgery and treatment are only for temporary demand. Whereas, the drugs consumed for healing and wellness are for the longer term. This is why medicines such as cholesterol-lowering drugs, anti-depressant drugs and health supplements are in great demand. It is small wonder that there is such enormous research material on the Internet on health matters. Hence the growing trend is for companies to target wellness as a business.

People fall sick through external viruses or attacks from external factors such as infectious diseases, and internal events such as heart disease. Companies get attacked by both external and internal viruses. The internal viruses are mainly management problems and generated internally. These external viruses include competition and economic and financial turmoil - namely factors from the outside.

Similarly, we will see an increased awareness for companies to target for corporate wellness. After many years of growth and change in the 2000's, companies have found that the state of health has not significantly improved. Morale and loyalty of the staff had deteriorated quickly in the destabilized economic market of late 2008, and companies became caught in a vicious cycle of restructuring to stay afloat. And this pressure to stay competitive is increasing with the continued downward spiral of the economy. Companies have found that it is better for them to stay well and healthy, as one does not have to get sick to get better.

There are workable preventive, diagnostic and therapeutic steps to treat sick companies, and to restore as well as maintain their well being. Similar to the handling of a person's health, a company needs to monitor the five stages to sustain long-term health and wellness, namely, prevention, early diagnosis, proper treatment, recovery or rehabilitation, and strengthening or health-boosting.

The issues affecting the health of a corporate entity parallel those for a human being; they are the preliminary, hard and soft issues. Preliminary issues are those matters that have to be right in the first place. For example, one needs to plan for one's physical and corporate health to prevent the onset of an ailment. In addition, the patient also needs to deal with the hard issues such as undergoing surgery to remove a tumour.

These hard issues are related to the "science" of the corporate wellness. There are also "soft issues" that the patient must be attuned to. These include strengthening the corporate culture, also known as the immune system of the body. The soft issues are like the "art" of the corporate wellness.

Studies show that the use of metaphors help people understand and retain information, as it acts as a framework to organize new information. However, the metaphor, as mentioned earlier, is merely a bridge to understand the concept; the sick companies have to cross that bridge.

PREVENTION

As the adage goes, "Prevention is better than cure." In medical practice, prevention of the disease before its onset is better than giving medication when it is already malignant or full-blown. Getting it right early is much better than subsequent expensive treatments.

Furthermore, when you lose your health, the road to recovery gets longer and rougher.

Prevention is the name of the game for individuals and companies. Just like people, most companies get into trouble simply through sheer neglect. Neglect has become the way of some businesses within the latter 2000's, including Fannie Mae and Freddie Mac, companies that, earlier in the game, would have benefited greatly from preventive medicine to avoid their later downfalls. Through the lack of monitoring, the accumulation of toxins or disease-causing pathogens are allowed to perpetuate into a full manifestation of the ailment before any action is taken to contain it. At the outset, a company should adopt prudent practices to prevent the onset of corporate ills or financial problems. The preliminary issue such as prevention requires the direction to be clear and also well-planned. Next, the hard issues need to be implemented which include diligent financial and other controls. Also, soft issues such as taking good care of your people and the wise management of the talent pool are also crucial.

DIAGNOSIS

Diagnosis is the identification of the disease based on its symptoms. However, the symptoms can sometimes mask the real disease. Also, many diseases share similar symptoms, thus further probing is required in order to ensure that the disease is not misdiagnosed.

Just as a sick person may manifest early symptoms of the ailment, such as cough, running nose, fever and body aches, likewise, there are usually ample warning signs for a company. High staff attrition rate and the loss of brand equity are perhaps some of the symptoms that all is not well with the company. However, they are merely the symptoms rather than the real disease or root cause. Treating the symptoms is tantamount to upgrading a cancer-stricken patient to another ward in the hospital; the condition of the patient does not improve. Prescription without diagnosis is malpractice, and likewise, implementing a corporate restructuring without knowing the root cause of the problems can be disastrous.

The key is early diagnosis, as it increases the chances of curing most diseases. Therefore, a company should put in place a detection system to facilitate this early diagnosis. How does a company get out of trouble? A good way is to diagnose how it gets into trouble in the first place.

Diagnosis starts with acknowledgement of the problem, good detection system and identifying the root causes from the symptom. Then one needs a comprehensive diagnosis of the "hard issues", such as its pricing, process and communication. The company also needs to review the "soft issues", such as communication and leadership functions, which may have got the company into trouble.

XXXX ' Corporate Turnaround Centre

TREATMENT

There are panaceas that can turn a critically ill organization into a healthy one; however, proper treatment is necessary as the remedies may be worse than the disease. For instance, some cancer patients are killed by the chemotherapy rather than the disease itself.

As they say, a stitch in time saves nine. Usually an ailing company needs critical attention probably in the form of 'surgery', with the primary focus of restructuring the organization and improving its cash flow. Most troubled companies need to engage outside help, encouraging change and drastic action to steer them out of the woods. Efforts are also needed to restore the company's bottom line and profits. Treatment starts with the execution in appointing the appropriate corporate doctor or turnaround manager or a team. Next, the distressed company needs to focus and understand some of the techniques to remedy its ailment. Hard issues take precedence during this stage with restructuring, right-sizing and cost-cutting. In some cases, the rescue endeavour may come in too late. If this is the case, then an exit strategy may be necessary. After dealing with the hard issues, the company needs to deal with the soft issues of dysfunctional personnel and bureaucracy.

RECOVERY

Once a company has completed its surgical care and come out of the 'intensive care' stage, it is of paramount importance that it continue to nurse itself to health. The pace of recovery and rehabilitation can vary from patients to patients, even though they may be afflicted by the same disease. Certainly the solution for saving AIG would not be the same as the one necessary to save Morgan-Stanley. Maintaining flexibility regarding recovery may be the difference between a successful recovery and a continued downward slide, especially in the current economically distressed environment of the late

XXXX ' Corporate Turnaround Centre

2000's.

Similar to the recovery after a surgery, a physiotherapist will start you on an exercise and rehabilitation regime such as assisting you to walk with crutches. As you recuperate in the hospital, the physiotherapist and occupational therapist will re-teach you the ways to walk, eat, bathe, sit and dress. They will also advise on your diet and exercise programs when you are discharged from hospital.

A company during this stage of the cycle needs to give itself time for healing and recovery. Then it needs to review and reflect on some of the hard issues relating to sales and marketing, and customers and market positioning. Oftentimes, these basic issues are taken for granted and can get the company into trouble even after drastic surgical issues have solved the more immediate needs. The recovery period is a good time for the company to recharge and re-energize itself through revisiting its ethical values, and inspirational and renewal processes.

STRENGTHENING

After full recovery, the battle to stay in good health is not over yet. The company needs to continue to strengthen and have foresight to transform and innovate. It must also continue to build up its cash reserves.

Some doctors believe that the immune system can defend the body against cancer and germs. The immunity is the defence system to combat diseases. During this phase, the strengthening of the immune system is the key to boosting health. The immune system for the company is the corporate culture. A dysfunctional corporate culture is one that is arrogant and full of ego. A company needs to strengthen its immune system through healthy mindsets and vision. In medical science of psychosomatics, it is believed that the mental health can affect the physical health; similarly the mindset of the company can hurt the financial health. Oftentimes, in a sick company, the enemy is within. An organization that has regained corporate wellness needs to implement a sustained program to remain in the pink of health. The company needs to strengthen its heart through exercise, good diet and vitamin supplements. As these are long-term measures, their benefits are normally not visible immediately.

Corporate Culture: Innovative, Fast and Flexible

Many organizations start out small and nimble, but as they grow, they slow down. Several causes may be at play. Adding a layer of management without the authority to act means adding gatekeepers...otherwise known as bottlenecks. Overly complex procedures, cover-your-tail and for-your-information memos, and the natural desire to preserve what has worked: all these conspire to stifle creativity and slow the pace of change.

In order to thrive, a corporate culture must have three characteristics: it must be innovative, fast and flexible.

Innovative companies constantly push to find improvements. They strive to improve the quality and reduce the cost of existing products, services and processes. And they measure their progress on an ongoing basis.

Fast-moving companies streamline processes so they can respond to change. Yes, contracts must be reviewed and signed. Yes, budgets must be proposed and approved. But periodic reviews of these processes will reveal that some are simply not needed or are being delayed by lower-priority activities.

Flexible companies can make changes "on the fly" in response to new or changing conditions.

Ultimate Corporate Transformation™ Index

The Ultimate Corporate Transformation Index™ (**UCTI**) uses two basic inputs:

- Productivity: Output divided by Input
- Innovation Culture Index is determined by following the **Innovation Culture in Ninety Questions** ™ tool, which measures your company's ability to innovatively implement productivity improvements and to productively implement new innovations

So the UCTI is the weighted product of the Productivity Index times the Innovation Culture Index.

For a company in Phase I, which is struggling for survival and using productivity gains to do so, the UCTI should be heavily weighted toward the Productivity Index. It may be difficult to muster the resources to measure the Innovation Culture Index at this time.

A company moving through Phase II should also move to balancing the UCTI more equally between Productivity and Innovation. One benchmark for beginning Phase II should be to gather the baseline statistics for the Innovation Culture Index.

In Phase III, which puts the focus on innovation, a company should put three-quarters of the weight on the Innovation Culture Index. By this time, ongoing productivity improvements should be engrained in the corporate culture. It becomes time to put the spotlight on innovation and creativity.

Innovation Culture in Ninety Questions

Introduction to the 90 Questions

High performance, consistent innovation, productivity and so many more qualities of successful organizations are not the results of "just luck". A successful and mature company has established systematic processes to ensure the best outcomes in each endeavour. The questions in this section help to identify whether your organization is well-prepared or whether it needs to improve.

Quality of Work

If management consultants present one recurring theme, it is "quality". Delivering high-quality products and services to customers has become a major competitive advantage for successful companies.

Quality may be measured as a percentage, usually in the form of "(Gross minus Defects) divided by Gross." If there are no defects, then the quality is 100%. If one-quarter of the "gross" are defective, then quality is 75%. Here are some examples:

- (Total number of products minus number of defective products) divided by the total number of products
- (Total cost of inputs minus cost of defects) divided by the total cost of inputs
- (Total value of products minus value of potential revenue lost due to defective products) divided by the total value of products

Remember that the Six Sigma process is named for a quality percentage: 99.99966%.

Problem Finders

Problem Finders are people who notice problems or bottlenecks, and if they cannot fix these issues themselves, will report recommendations to

XXXX' Corporate Turnaround Centre

management. Others may find ways to make improvements – possibly changing something from "very good" to "excellent." Some people are inclined by their nature to notice things that need to be improved. But does your organization think of them as "agents of change" or as "trouble-makers"?

Harness and channel the energies of the Problem Finders so that they benefit your company. Develop processes to elicit and respond to problems – before they affect your customers.

Organizational Resources for Innovators

Innovation is crucial for the long-term success of an organization. The world around you will change; will you make changes, adapt to changes, or be overwhelmed by changes?

An organization must nurture and support its innovative employees with appropriate resources and infrastructure. These resources include budgets for time, labour, and materials; access to information; and support from management.

Organizational Infrastructure

Employees cannot work toward unknown goals. Senior management must develop communication channels to share goals and strategies, and to learn what the rank-and-file are thinking.

The infrastructure must support the goals. A hospital's operating room must be very clean to minimize the risk of infection. Cutting costs for disinfectants and cleaning will likely result in higher post-operative treatment costs. Similar logic works for any organization: identify the desired results; determine what is required to attain those results; then apply appropriate resources to achieve those results. Budget for the effort to maintain your organization's infrastructure: bricks and mortar; tools and equipment; policies and procedures.

Rules and Regulations

Every company has rules, but must find the balance between flexibility and enforcement. Banks cannot permit lax or corrupt accounting practices; but should they be flexible in lending to small businesses?

It can be difficult to distinguish absolute requirements and helpful procedures, or the difference between the means and the goal. For example, it may be absolutely necessary to have a customer's signature on an invoice, but a FAX transmission may be an acceptable alternative to hand-delivery of the original document.

Leadership

How well the management team works with other employees is critical for the company's success. Is there clear, effective, two-way communication? Have managers earned the respect of the workforce? Senior management is responsible for formulating and communicating strategy, and for setting the direction of the organization. Do the leaders pay attention to how, and how well, they communicate?

Is the management team *pro-active* in seeking and developing new opportunities? Or do they *react* in response to external challenges? Do they ensure high competence in core business activities?

Creativity

Innovation will not take place in a company that strangles creativity in its crib, or allows it to die of neglect. Foster and nourish the innovators in your organization.

Failure

Nurturing successful innovators cannot succeed if there is a price for failure. Employees will notice whether failure is punished or is treated as a learning opportunity. Thomas Edison considered that his many failures to find a filament for the light bulb were simply steps along the path to success.

Performance of Individuals:

An individual employee will perform better if he or she knows that the work will be noticed. Don't allow people to hide in teams. Review individual performance and provide appropriate feedback. That is not to say that teamwork is irrelevant, but an individual's performance as a team member is still, largely, that person's responsibility.

Management must lead by example in taking responsibility for their performance, and for setting and maintaining processes to spotlight each individual as the important and valuable contributors that they are.

Individual Contributions:

Involving front-line employees in a variety of roles is an important way of keeping everyone aware of the big picture.

One story from NASA says it best. A variety of NASA employees were asked about their jobs. The answers included: "engine design"; "propellant storage"; "telemetry"; and "mission planning." But one janitor, leaning on his mop, replied "I help send people into space."

Recognize the achievements of individuals. Encourage people to take responsibility, to work hard, and to make positive contributions. This encouragement may take on many forms, such as token or financial recognition; promotion; or a write-up in a corporate bulletin.

News media often report on CEO compensation. Well, the CEO is also an individual – someone who succeeds in this high-profile role deserves to be recognized too.

These questions will focus mainly on individual contributions towards creativity and innovation.

Role of the Organization:

The company has a role in nurturing and developing the skills and talents of its employees. This can take on many forms: training specific skills; encouraging formal education; providing "stretch" opportunities; and rewarding individuals for learning and achieving new things.

Conversely, the organization may stifle individuals by refusing to recognise new skills, and by punishing those who take risks.

The External Environment

The external environment refers to factors outside your company, that form the environment in which your organization operates and competes. Pharmaceutical firms, for example, may be subject to stricter governmental regulations than textile manufacturers. However, textile firms may face greater competitive pressures because it is easier for new companies to start production, as compared to drug manufacturing. The general economy plays a part; so do interest rates and lending practices.

The external environment may render some work obsolete. When the automobile came into its own as a means of transportation, the time for innovations in making horseshoes was at an end. The need for innovative ways of working with metal, however, was about to increase exponentially.

Outside conditions may challenge your organization. Has a competitor released a new product or outsourced for cheaper labour? Have new government regulations or higher interest rates blown holes in your business plan? Has a cheaper supplier stolen your loyal customers? Have they gone to a different product altogether? These environmental changes have forced some companies into bankruptcy. Your survival might depend on your well-practiced skills for innovation.

Responding to the problems of individuals

The phrase, "Do not shoot the messenger", is required because we have a tendency to vent frustration at the "bearer of bad news".

Challenges and setbacks are inevitable. Fostering effective habits of dealing with challenges will enable an organization to make corrections, to learn, and to improve.

An individual who is facing difficulties will perform less well than one not distracted by problems. The company can either support that individual or leave him or her to flounder. Which course of action does your organization take? Are there policies and procedures to ensure that individuals get the help they need?

Rules and Regulations

Innovators must "think outside the box" in order to create an invention. This leads to tension between those who hold the rulebook and those who want to play a different game altogether. Striking an appropriate balance is vital: which rules are necessary; which apply only in certain situations? Ignoring the need for discipline – for example, when a safety protocol is violated – incurs serious risks. Harsh discipline, especially for trying a new procedure which innovatively leads to better outcomes, will stifle creative minds.

XXXX ' Corporate Turnaround Centre

Quality of Work:

1. Does the organization support quality in any of the following ways: Does management teach the consequences of low-quality work versus high-quality work? Does the organization regularly state the need for high-quality work? Does management train staff to measure and improve quality?

2. Do the quality improvement programs contribute to the success of the organization?

Problem Finders:

3. Has the organization taken any steps or promoted any practices to identify Problem Finders?

4. Does any methodology exist to report on the output (results) of these Problem Finders from their reports, through management response, and to final resolution?

5. Does the organization provide resources or funds, affirmation or support to the Problem Finders?

Organizational Resources for Innovators:

6. Does the organization possess enough resources to support innovators?

7. Are basic facilities like office equipment available to the innovators?

8. Do the innovators have access to the business-related issues of the organization?

Organizational Infrastructure:

9. Do the employees know and understand the purposes and the objectives of the organization?

10. Do the employees make strategic plans to accomplish the tasks of the organization?

11. Does the infrastructure of the organization meet the needs of customers?

12. Is there a favourable environment for the workers to operate in the organization?
13. Is there any system to support risk policies?
14. Is there effective communication at all levels of the organization?
15. Does the organization give attention and priority to meeting customer needs?

Rules and Regulations:
16. Is the organization flexible in terms of adopting new rules and procedures in its framework?
17. Does the organization give freedom to the employees to create new innovative ideas?
18. Does the organization use the experiences of other organizations to develop and enforce its rules and regulations?
19. Does the organization have well-defined rules for making specific decisions at the appropriate levels?
20. Does the organization reward success and avoid punishing reasonable but unsuccessful innovations?

Leadership:
21. Do the leaders actively respond to changes in the organization?
22. Does management address initiatives proposed by individuals?
23. Do leaders regularly communicate with the employees of the organization?
24. Does the management respond positively to the concerns of the employees?
25. Are there any effective procedures to resolve the problems of the employees?
26. Does management spend time developing and promoting new ideas?
27. Does management adopt the methodology for knowledge management in their organization, to effectively share knowledge?

28. Does the management regularly introduce new technologies?
29. Does the management promote innovation?
30. Does management adopt risk-taking strategies to further the interests of the organization?
31. Has management developed clear aims and objectives?
32. Does management make the decisions effectively?
33. Do employees show confidence and trust in management's decisions?
34. Does management take proper action when a problem is reported?
35. Do you consider management's decision-making performance to be "excellent"?

Creativity:
36. Does management support creative activities in the organization?
37. Has management adopted specific procedures to deal with creative activities?
38. Does management provide funds to support these constructive activities?

Failure:
39. Does the organization tolerate failure due to (approved) innovations? (For example: providing leeway in a call centre script may be informal, whereas R&D projects are formal).
40. Does the organization follow a process to learn from a failure?
41. Does the management possess the calibre to overcome failure?
42. Does management encourage the efforts of individuals to overcome failure?

Performance of Individuals:

43. Do individuals within the organization perform effectively?
44. Does management encourage the efforts of individuals?
45. Does management reward the performance of individuals?
46 Does management provide support to the individuals to create new plans or initiatives?

47. Does management provide funds for individuals to take part in innovative activities? (3M and Google are examples).
48. Does management concentrate on providing opportunities to individuals?
49. Does the management tolerate an individual's failure when applying an (approved) innovation?
50. Does management follow a process to learn from the failures and success of the individuals?

Individual creativity and innovation

51. Are individuals permitted or encouraged to contribute creatively to the success of the company?
52. Do individuals try to contribute creatively in all the fields and aspects of the company?
53. Do innovations proposed or developed by individuals play any role in getting a positive outcome?
54. Do individuals regularly suggest innovations related to the marketing and selling of products?
55. Do individuals take part in the matters concerned with innovation in processes and procedures?
56. Do individuals regularly suggest and participate in research-related activities?
57. Are individuals committed to improving the results of the organization?
58. Are individuals committed to introducing new innovative activities like knowledge transfer?
59. Have individuals made any great innovative contributions up to now?
60. Are individuals effective in suggesting and introducing innovations to the organization?
61. Were there occasions in the history of the organization where an individual's innovations played a destructive role for the organization?

XXXX ' Corporate Turnaround Centre

Role of the Organization:

62. Does the organization provide any funds to support the innovative activities of individuals?

63. Does the organization launch initiatives to support the activities of individuals?

64. Does the organization understand the role of knowledge management to transfer the knowledge among individuals?

65. Does the organization have a special frame-work for controlling the activities of individuals?

66. Does the organization consider the role of individuals in the success of the organization?

67. Does the organization conduct seminars to teach the individuals about new projects?

68. Does the organization have any system or metric for measuring the productivity of the individuals?

69. Does the organization reward the individuals for extra-ordinary work?

70. Does the organization get expert assistance to enhance the activities of the individuals?

71. Does the organization tolerate a failure of an individual when applying an (approved) innovation? (This may include formal R&D projects or informally-approved variations on standard work practices).

72. Has the organization introduced any initiatives to educate individuals, whether in-house training or subsidizing college studies or certification programs

73. Does the organization keep records of extra-ordinary performances of individuals?

74. Does the organization provide funds to individuals for exploring new ideas?

Internal and External Environments:

75. Is the internal physical environment (including the work space, tools and equipment, and other resources) suitable for the activities of the individuals?

76. Is the corporate and physical environment (including the corporate culture, work space and other resources) suitable for the transfer of knowledge among the individuals?

77. Is the external competitive environment suitable for bringing new initiatives for enhancing the activities of individuals, or is corporate survival the only relevant goal at this time?

78. Is either the internal corporate environment or the external competitive environment suitable for individuals to achieve some significant successes through creative innovations?

79. What metrics have been introduced to measure the suitability of either the internal corporate environment or the external competitive environment?

Response to difficulties:

80. Does the organization have a systematic and supportive methodology to respond when an individual has a problem?

81. How much time does management take before answering the questions of individuals?

82. Does the management respond properly to the problems of individuals?

83. Does management give tips or training to individuals in order to meet their goals?

84. Does a manager consult with individuals in implementing changes?

85. Does management use a systematic approach to the individuals in dealing with major issues?

Rules and Regulations:

86. Do the rules and regulations of the organization support the work of the individuals?

87. Does management take corrective actions if the individuals violate the rules and regulations?

88. Do the individuals obey the rules and regulations of the organization?

89. Do the individuals follow any specific rules for achieving their goals?

90. Does management concentrate on disciplining individuals who disobey rules?

END OF MODULE #9

The application of spiritual principles to your company's turnaround is complete. It is time to think about you yourself. The turnaround CEO must not neglect his or her own health in the process of saving the company. In the next module, we finish this Toolkit by looking at how to "turn yourself around": **self-transformation**.

~

Additional Online Resources

The following books authored by Dr. Mike Teng are relevant to this module, covering Corporate Wellness. Details are available by clicking on the website below for each book.

Corporate Wellness: 101 principles in turnaround and transformation and other transformation package

www.corporateturnaroundexpert.com

"Increase Your Profits by 107% in 9 months Using 27 years of Time-Tested East-West Strategies. Use of 3 Simple Steps."

Training Manual: Corporate turnaround and transformation methodology

www.turnaroundmethodology.com

A comprehensive and ultimate corporate turnaround methodology is one that combines the best practices from the West and the East, soundly transforming troubled companies into industry leaders.

Corporate Wellness: Spiritual and secular principles in corporate turnaround and transformation

www.turnaroundservice.com

By understanding the principles contained in this book, you can save your company – it's as simple as that! Don't wait until you're filing for bankruptcy to believe that corporate wellness is the foundation from which the success of a company is built.

Turnaround Toolkit

www.turnaroundhandbook.com

This is a comprehensive toolkit with all the resources necessary for corporate transformation and turnaround. It covers from strategy from the tactical right down to the individual level.

You can also visit Dr. Mike Teng's www.youtube.com/1103teng **to watch the YouTube videos of some of the books.**

http://www.youtube.com/watch?v=w0PGk2qbedM**Corporate Wellness: Spiritual and secular principles in corporate turnaround and transformation**
http://tinyurl.com/corporatewellness
Sick companies are failing everywhere! Your corporation wellness is surely falling during this second great depression. Is your firm in desperate need of a turnaround? Are you facing a dramatic change in your company's profit margin due to poor management? Is the world-wide economic depression causing you to rethink your corporate strategy? Is there any way to save your firm and ensure a healthy future?

Ultimate Corporate Turnaround and Transformation Methodology
http://tinyurl.com/turnaroundmethodology
The 3-Step turnaround is as follows:
Step 1: Surgery improves your cash flow by restructuring the organization and putting a stop to the unnecessary expenses.
Step 2: Resuscitation injects new business income streams and boosts existing sales to increase your profits.
Step 3: Therapy strengthens your corporate culture and team to build a strong and healthy corporate immune system to sustain long-term growth

Turnaround Handbook
http://tinyurl.com/turnaroundhandbook
Did your company take a beating in the recent fall of the global stock market, or do you stay awake at night worrying about how your company can expand into Asia and become a prominent player in the Asian Century? Are you overburdened with the stress of not knowing how to motivate your teams, keep up with changing technology, counter the slowdown in the U.S. economy,

or remain competitive in a fast-moving business environment? If you answered yes to any of these questions, then read on, because I have the ultimate solution for all of your corporate financial problems. You have been dreaming of turning your company from an ailing giant headed toward bankruptcy into a healthy, robust company that is more profitable than ever, and today I am offering you the complete toolkit to do exactly that.

MODULE #10

TRANSFORM

YOURSELF:

CHANGING MINDSET

INTRODUCTION: "Turn Yourself Around"

Are we approaching the Second Great Depression? Now, history seems to be repeating itself, as the recent economic scenario indicates. Renowned financial institutions in the USA and other developed countries have brought themselves to a state of near collapse or total bankruptcy due to their reckless lending in the name of home mortgage loans. Some of them can survive, but at the cost of writing off their losses, while others do not even have enough capital to cover their losses, and will have to wind up!

Thus, the imminent consequences of what is happening in the world today are there for all to see: rising unemployment rate, downsizing, increased stress, and possibly even suicides.

The question that will be uppermost in your mind in these changing circumstances is, "How long am I safe"? Because let us not forget - what affects the Americans affects the rest of the world too! We are all globally interlinked. So, your inner mentality cannot stay immune to whatever is happening in your external environment for very long. It therefore becomes even more imperative now that you create such a strong shield of positivism and courage around you that nothing can faze you!

The next image shows how personal transformation – "Turnaround Yourself" – starts from the core of your being and works outward to your relationships.

XXXX ' Corporate Turnaround Centre

Turnaround Yourself

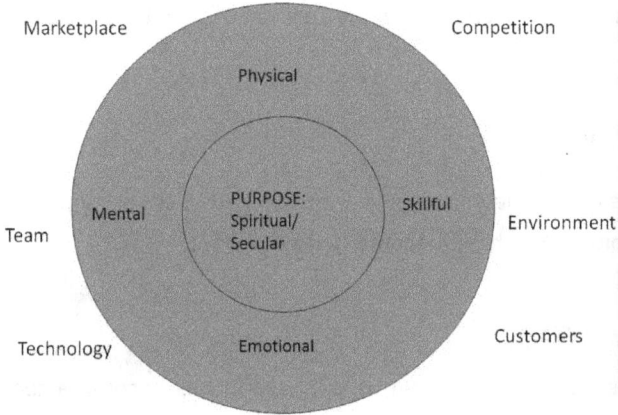

MANAGING YOURSELF AWAY FROM STRESS

The following indicators of stress might be of help to you to identify how stressed out you are.

Sign #1:

Sudden spurts of anger directed at family members, close friends, colleagues at work, etc. Reflecting back on those incidents, you would discover that there really was no cause for your anger; you just felt like "letting go."

XXXX ' Corporate Turnaround Centre

Sign #2:

You wish to withdraw from routine leisure activities that you enjoyed previously. You have begun to feel that they take time away from "useful work."

Sign #3:

Depression, anxiety, nagging worries and lack of happiness are your new companions. You have become hypersensitive.

Sign #4:

Sleeplessness accompanied by exhaustion has become a regular phenomenon for you at night. All those negative thoughts refuse to let you relax.

Sign #5:

People who found you approachable in the past stay away, since your irritation and ever-changing moods irk them. They never know what to expect from you.

Sign #6:

Do you experience mood swings often? Do you hate criticism, and feel that the whole world is against you? Then, you are definitely heading for a "burnout"!

Sign #7:

Your levels of concentration and attentiveness are at an all-time low. Your work stays incomplete because you are feeling overwhelmed by how much you have to accomplish.

Sign #8:

You feel lonely and alienated. Your socializing comes down drastically.

XXXX ' Corporate Turnaround Centre

The above-mentioned signs are psychological. Physiological signs also make an appearance. These include: tension headaches, high blood pressure, muscle aches and pains, chest pain, heartburn, stomach ailments, nervous behaviours, etc.

It is very important for you to realize that stress is not always a negative factor. If taken in a positive manner, it can be a very positive catalyst for you, because it brings out the best in you in critical situations. But you still need to build up those tension-coping reserves. To do this and to ensure that stress does not get the better of you, it would be advisable to practice stress management techniques like exercise and prayers. A disciplined life with healthy food habits, plenty of fresh air and exercise, and a positive attitude should go a long way in ensuring a stress-free lifestyle.

Prayers and meditation give you happiness and freedom from stress. The benefits extend to your mind also; in fact, harmony between mind and body is achieved through prayer. You are relieved because you put your burden on the shoulders of a more supreme being than yourself. The achievements of a positive outlook and serenity aid in bringing balance to a mind tormented by conflicts and confusion.

If you cannot devote sufficient time and discipline to prayers and meditation, then you can develop the daily habit of going for a short walk. Communing with nature and getting plenty of fresh air will clear the mind of any cobwebs that might be present. Of course, healthy nutrition is not to be forgotten because of greater concentration on exercise!

An old Chinese adage states: "The glory is not in ever failing, but in rising every time you fall." So, only when you firmly make up your mind to go in for a complete turnaround or transformation, will you develop this ability to face all setbacks and adverse conditions with fortitude.

XXXX ' Corporate Turnaround Centre

You may go to umpteen counselors and sign up for numerous courses on personality development, but do bear in mind that you are your own best counsellor. Your subconscious mind can bring about such phenomenal internal changes that tackling harsh extraneous circumstances will seem like child's play to you!

Getting into the habit of sharing your stressful experiences with people who care to listen, like family, spouse, close friends, trusted relatives, therapists, and even understanding neighbours can help you unburden your mind. Relaxation and sleep are very important to counter stress and it is vital for everyone to remember the relations and strengths in our lives which in usual times we take for granted.

EXERCISE 10.1

ARE YOU CLEAR ABOUT YOURSELF?

The signs in the table below are psychological and physiological indicators that you may be stressed. Consider yourself and rate each sign either "high", "medium" or "low" for severity and frequency.

Potential Signs of Stress		Severity (High, Medium, Low)	Frequency (High, Medium, Low)
Psychological	Sudden spurts of anger directed at family members, close friends, colleagues at work, etc.		
	You wish to withdraw from routine leisure activities that you enjoyed previously. You have begun to feel that they take time away from "useful work."		
	Depression, anxiety, nagging worries and lack of happiness are your new companions. You have become hypersensitive.		
	Sleeplessness accompanied by exhaustion has become a regular phenomenon for you at night. All those negative thoughts refuse to let you relax.		
	People who found you approachable in the past stay away, since your irritation and ever-changing moods irk them. They never know what to expect from you.		
	Do you experience mood swings often? Do you hate criticism, and feel that the whole world is against you?		
	Your levels of concentration and attentiveness are at an all-time low. Your work stays incomplete because you are feeling overwhelmed by how much you have to accomplish.		
	You feel lonely and alienated. Your socializing comes down drastically.		
Physiological	Tension headaches		
	High blood pressure		
	Muscle aches and pains		
	Chest pain		
	Heartburn		
	Stomach ailments		
	Nervous behaviours		

XXXX ' Corporate Turnaround Centre

SIX STRATEGIES TO TRANSFORM YOURSELF

Now I will try to present some additional strategies that can help you in managing your stress. I'm sure these strategies will help you in turning around and achieving your goal.

(1) How Your Faith Can Help You

"FAITH" is a five-letter word that carries a wealth of meaning. You can make this magical word a part of your life if you wish to achieve success, for it is faith in your own abilities that can take you to new heights and help you fulfil all your desired goals. It bestows a mysterious power that aids in overcoming all sorts of hurdles in life. If you don't believe in your abilities in times of crisis, then who else will?

Of course, you can be your own faith builder or be your own faith stealer. Let me explain further. If you find these qualities within yourself: constantly worrying, doubting or being obsessed with negative thoughts, then you are allowing yourself to become a faith stealer. And you will prove to be a negative influence on people around you too! But if you develop the qualities of peace, prayer, and trust, you are on the way to becoming a faith builder not only in yourself, but in others!

(2) Support of Family and Friends

For any individual, the greatest amount of moral and emotional support is received from family and friends. Without them around, you would really feel like an empty shell, for even if the whole world is against you, they would stand by you simply because they have immense faith in you! Your friends, in fact, can even prove to be more objective and optimistic than close family members at times. It therefore becomes easy to overcome the worst of hurdles. You cannot choose your family members, but you can choose your friends! Thus, it's important that you talk to the optimistic, the positive-minded people around you! The people who love you will be forthright in pointing out your strengths and weaknesses. This helps you focus better, and achieve that turnaround in your personality that you always wanted! After all, you were brought into this world to be the best "YOU" that you can be!

Therefore, always show care, concern, and gratitude, and you will receive the same in return. And when you carry this attitude over to your work place, it will create a healthier work environment.

(3) Impact of Upbringing

Why is it said that you are what your environment makes you? It is because your upbringing shapes the way your thought process works and how you handle day-to-day situations. If you have been brought up in a safe, warm and loving household, it is but natural that strong familial bonds will give you the courage to face any situation that may arise – be it at school, college or at the work place. Trust in oneself, fortitude and patience, and people skills will all come naturally.

But does this mean that if you were not fortunate enough to have a good upbringing, you will turn out to be a coward, a criminal, etc.? Does it mean that you have no right to be happy? Absolutely not! You obviously had no control over the way you were brought up, but now you have the power to decide what your future is going to be like. Of course, moving away from what is familiar and taking a turnaround to step into an unfamiliar world is not easy, but it is only when you "nurture" yourself that you will find true happiness. You are the creator of your own destiny!

(4) Culture and Values

As a leader of your team, you are responsible, along with many others, in shaping the work culture and values of your organization. As a matter of fact, it is your own personal values that will carry over into your organization and help shape its work culture. Your upbringing and training will determine whether you can learn to respect your co-workers or not, despite differences of opinion at times. Will you allow autonomy in decision-making? How credible and trustworthy are you? In fact, your conduct at your work place depends on your culture and values. And in case you discover that certain values are negative, be prepared to un-learn them! Be ready to adopt new and positive values too.

(5) These People Made it to the Top after Losing

History books are full of tales about famous people who fought against all odds to make it big in their lives. These people were not bothered by the adversities they faced, as they had a deep hunger to accomplish something great.

(6) Other factors

You will not always face one problem at one time; sometimes, several crop up together. It is then that you find yourself in a dilemma. So, study all of them carefully, work out all the aspects and solutions for each, and prioritize them. By this, I mean that there are some issues that need immediate handling so take care of them first. The others can be relegated to the background for some time, at least until you are able to fix them. Trying to deal with all of them at once may lead to a nervous breakdown! So, be careful!

What you need to learn and realize here is that running away from your problems is no solution. There is a much better way to face your problems and find a solution. It is a great idea to turn around and face what's tough. Every problem has a set of solutions and you can always find the right one.

As you can see above, defeat and setbacks are stepping stones for achievement in life. Each setback that comes your way – be it in your career, your personal life or even an economic recession – if taken in the right spirit, will shake you out of your comfort zone and force you to rethink your strategy using a new perspective, innovatively, efficiently, and more purposefully. It brings out facets of your life that you never even knew existed or that you were capable of. Keeping the faith on the way will be the compass needle that will guide you through the difficult times.

EXERCISE 10.2

TURN IT ALL AROUND

Consider these turnaround strategies and then identify your personal turnaround actions.

Your Faith Can Help You:
- Be your own faith builder with peace, prayer, and trust.

Support of Family and Friends:
- Show and receive care, concern, and gratitude from your family and friends.

Impact of Upbringing:
- Make the most of the positive aspects of your upbringing and also "nurture" yourself in order to find true happiness.

Culture and Values:
- Consider your own personal values and be prepared to un-learn any negative ones. Be ready to adopt new and positive values too.

These People Made It to the Top After Losing:
1. Consider the examples of others.

My personal turnaround actions		
Short-term	**Medium-term**	**Long-term**

EXERCISE 10.3

DEVELOPMENT PLAN

1. Identify your strengths and areas for development.
2. Write down your goals.
3. Specify resources and strategies.
4. Make a timeline.
5. Document your progress and accomplishments.
6. Review your progress and accomplishments with others.

My personal development plan		
Strengths	**Areas for development**	**Goals**
Resources	**Strategies**	**Timeline**
Progress	**Accomplishments**	**Reviewed?**

XXXX ' Corporate Turnaround Centre

END OF MODULE #10

Your journey of analysis and planning is complete. You have everything you need to turnaround your company and yourself. Good luck!

Well, everything except some practical, real-world examples. Please see the case studies in the next chapter.

~

Additional Online Resources

The following book authored by Dr. Mike Teng is relevant to this module, covering Turnaround Yourself. Details are available by clicking on the website below.

Turnaround Yourself: How to get out of depression during the second great depression

www.turnaroundyourself.com

This unique book can get you back on track so that you are happy, healthy and emotionally stable again.

You can also visit Dr. Mike Teng's www.youtube.com/1103teng **to watch the YouTube videos of the book.**

Turnaround yourself: Getting Out of the Depression during the Second Great Depression

http://tinyurl.com/turnaroundyourself

History has taught us quite a few things about the first Great Depression, but apparently it has not taught us enough. The global economy is in recession again and we can all see history repeating itself. Unemployment, business failures, bankruptcies, loss of property and foreclosures are just some of the consequences of a serious global depression. Turning ourselves around is the solution to getting out of this great depression.

MODULES #11 & #12

PRACTICAL SESSIONS

290   XXXX ' Corporate Turnaround Centre

Forums with industry practitioners who understand the EPI-ECO Transformation Methodology

Submission of practical cases in the field

3 Phases of Singapore Economic Transformation

	Surgery: Productivity 1960 – 1980		Resuscitation: Prod/Innovation 1980 - 2000		Therapy: Innovation 2000 - Present	
Operation	1.	Employer friendly laws	1.	Tripartite arrangement	1.	Foreign talent attraction
	2.	Compete on low labour costs – electronics industry	2.	Grow IT intensive industry	2.	Promote R&D - Biotech industry
Strategy	1.	Attract labour intensive industries	1.	Attract hi-tech industries	1.	Attract knowledge based industries
	2.	Create low-paying jobs to keep unemployment down	2.	Create high value added jobs to increase wages	2.	Create SMEs, entrepreneurs to replace departing MNCs
Culture	1.	Government led	1.	Government/ Private sector led	1.	Private sector led
	2.	Manufacturing biased	2.	Manufacturing/ Service biased	2.	Service biased – integrated resorts

XXXX ' Corporate Turnaround Centre

Questions for the Case Study on Singapore

1. Discuss the different challenges that faced Singapore during each of the phases.
2. How did Singapore leverage its assets in each phase?
3. Discuss the strategies used in each phase.

SUMMARY

&

CONCLUSION

"Turnaround Yourself"

A financial tsunami has come our way,

That threatens to do us no good,

Destroying companies and washing our jobs away,

Leaving a mess where a factory once stood.

Talents are not enough to survive,

And save the many corporate lives

It is how we turn around ourselves,

So that we can help others to energise themselves.

Whatever our difficult business line,

Whatever our financial pain,

There will be economic sunshine,

After the tsunami rain.

Perhaps we may fall,

Perhaps we may not last,

But God is always for all,

To help us through this bust

XXXX' Corporate Turnaround Centre

A COMPARATIVE SUMMARY

This table offers a snapshot, easy reference comparison of the different approaches needed in each of the three turnaround phases:

	Phase I Surgery	Phase II Resuscitation	Phase III Therapy
Leadership Style	Transactional	Transactional/ Transformational	Transformational
Managerial Type	Benevolent	Coaching	Spiritual
Communication Mode	Close/Didactic	Didactic	Open/Interactive
Viral Treatment	Internal Viruses	Internal/External Viruses	Internal/External Viruses
Intensive Care Unit	In ICU	Partially out of ICU	Out of ICU
Management	Hard/Brain issues	Hard/Brain Issues/Soft Issues	Soft/Heart Issues

This summary is best seen as a graduated spectrum from Phase I to Phase III. For instance, the primary financial emphasis in Phase I is on cash flow, moving on to revenues, profits and cash flow in Phase II and subsequently to sustainable revenues, profits and cash flow in Phase III.

This is partly dictated by the short time-frame (a few months) in Phase I, medium time-frame (less than one year) in Phase II and longer (more than one year) time-frame in Phase III.

Adjustments to corporate orientation also move from Focus (Phase I) to Focus and Fast (Phase II) and eventually to Focus, Fast and Flexible (Phase III) as the primary target(s) of the company's viral treatment gravitates from Internal Viruses (Phase I) to both Internal and External Viruses (Phases II and III).

CONCLUDING REMARKS

Without doubt, the corporate turnaround experience is a very trying yet immensely rewarding one. The satisfaction of being able to nurse an ailing company back to the pink of health is indescribable. The ability to change lives and make a difference to others is gratifying and cannot be measured in monetary terms. At the end of the day, corporate turnaround is not a miracle but sheer hard work and going back to the basics.

This **Transformation Toolkit** brings together the fruits of my experience and insights and learning as a Turnaround CEO. It merges my corporate turnaround methodology with my observations on Corporate Wellness, Office Politics and – possibly most importantly of all these days – Ultimate Internet Marketing. I hope that this Toolkit has helped guide you through the process of turning your company around and creating a healthy future.

Thank you.

www.ingramcontent.com/pod-product-compliance
Lightning Source LLC
Chambersburg PA
CBHW052107230326
41599CB00054B/4283